OVERCOMING *The* ADVERSARY

Warfare Praying Against
Demon Activity

MARK I. BUBECK

OVERCOMING *The* ADVERSARY

Warfare Praying Against
Demon Activity

MARK I. BUBECK

MOODY PUBLISHERS
CHICAGO

Library of Congress Cataloging in Publication Data

Bubeck, Mark I.
Overcoming the Adversary.
1. Christian life—Baptist authors. 2. Devil. I. Title

BV4501.2.B817 1984 248.4´861 84-1943

ISBN: 978-0-8024-0333-9

We hope you enjoy this book from Moody Publishers. Our goal is to provide high-quality, thought-provoking books and products that connect truth to your real needs and challenges. For more information on other books and products written and produced from a biblical perspective, go to www.moodypublishers.com or write to:

Moody Publishers
820 N. LaSalle Boulevard
Chicago, IL 60610

29 30

Printed in the United States of America

To those many people who have shared with me their personal battles in spiritual warfare. Through their sufferings and victories, I have been encouraged by the Lord to engage in the study and effort necessary to complete this book.

Contents

Preface

"I have set the Lord always before me. Because he is at my right hand, I will not be shaken" (Psalm 16:8).

"Cast your cares on the Lord and he will sustain you; he will never let the righteous fall" (Psalm 55:22).

"I can do everything through him who gives me strength" (Philippians 4:13).

Both the Old and New Testaments convey to us that there is a secure, immovable, invincible place of victory for God's people. It is God's plan that those who belong to Christ will always be able to do God's will. No enemy can interfere with that plan unless the believer allows that enemy to rob him of his victorious stance. The purpose of this book is to help believers grasp a prayer practice that will enable them to walk in victory.

The reader will find reference made from time to time to my book *The Adversary.* This present volume, *Overcoming the Adversary,* is a sequel to *The Adversary.* It was written in response to many requests for an additional, practical "handbook" for spiritual warfare.

The emphasis of this book is prayer, a discipline that is often disgracefully neglected among evangelical Christians. One report has indicated that even "the average pastor surveyed prays only three minutes each day."[1] If that presents even a partial picture of what is happening in the prayer life of the church, we are in serious trouble.

The following call of Andrew Murray needs to be heeded today:

> A most important phase of prayer is intercession. What a work God has set open for those who are His priests—intercessors! We find a

1. *Christianity Today,* 6 April 1979, 52.

> wonderful expression in the prophecy of Isaiah; God says, "Let him take hold of me;" and again, "There is none that stirreth up himself to take hold of thee." In other passages God refers to the intercessors for Israel. Have you ever taken hold of God? The church and the world need nothing so much as a mighty Spirit of intercession to bring down the power of God on earth. Pray for the descent from heaven of the Spirit of intercession for a great prayer revival.[2]

It is my desire that this book should awaken the reader to the awesome resource of prayer.

My deepest appreciation goes to my devoted wife, Anita, for her time and effort expended in helping complete this project. Special thanks to Rose, Gladys, and Donna for their labor of love in the typing and retyping of the manuscript. I must also express my profound appreciation to the Central Baptist Church family for their encouragement, prayers, and patience so lovingly extended as I worked on this book. The life and strength of the body of believers was very supportive of the task.

2. Charles Cook, ed. *Daily Meditations for Prayer* (Westchester, Ill.: Good News, n.d.), 330.

Introduction

As she came into my office, her eyes brimmed with tears, and her moist hands betrayed her anxiety. Her voice had the same quiver of fear I had noted when she had called for an appointment. Nancy* was the daughter of missionaries, a brilliant student, and a beautiful nineteen-year-old.

After a few moments of prayer, she opened her heart. "Pastor Bubeck, I've been tormented for several months now. Almost every night when I try to sleep, the sense of a fearful presence seems to close in on me. I've even seen ghostlike apparitions in my room, and I'm so afraid."

Nancy's problem had started when she and some of her classmates at a Christian college had seen the film *The Exorcist.* Since that time her torments had come with varying intensity. She wanted to know where she could find help. How could she be free from this fear? Was her anxiety purely psychological—was she losing her mind? Or could it be that Satan or his demons were causing her problem? If so, what could she do?

I tried to show Nancy some of the principles for spiritual warfare set forth in the Word of God. New insights, and with them renewed confidence, began to build in her heart. As she saw her victory in the Lord Jesus Christ, some of the fear began to drain away.

Nancy's problem is a growing one in the church today. Before she left my office she asked a question that deserves an answer. "I'm seeing a whole new side to the Christian life that I've never seen before. Why is it that in the nineteen years of my life I've scarcely

*Names of individuals used as examples in this book have been changed to protect their privacy.

heard about spiritual warfare?" I thought I detected a note of resentment, as though she felt cheated as a Christian.

A number of believers want an answer to that question. Why all of this renewed interest in Christian circles concerning demons and Satan's work? Is it just another passing fad? Does it center too much attention on the devil? Is it a subtle attempt of Satan to turn believers away from the important work of evangelism?

Satan's work certainly is not a passing fad. He has always hated all believers with a "cruel hatred." Satan's kingdom is engaged in a relentless effort to destroy Christians and their effective fulfillment of the will of God. There are several reasons the battle is becoming more open today.

One reason for increased overt activity of Satan in the lives of Christians is that until recently the subject of aggressive spiritual warfare has been largely neglected in evangelical circles. For the last seventy-five years most believers in America were lulled into an attitude of passively assuming their victory over Satan instead of aggressively applying it. When the Lord first led me into a deeper study of how the believer defeats Satan's power, I discovered that most of the sound doctrinal books written on the subject were very old. Evangelical seminaries and Bible schools had prepared their graduates to battle for the fundamentals of the faith but had provided little insight into how to engage in battle with Satan, a personal enemy.

Another reason we are seeing the battle more clearly is that we are living in the last days. First Timothy 4:1 declares: "The Spirit clearly says that in later times some will abandon the faith and follow deceiving spirits and things taught by demons." Such verses in the Word are to be taken soberly. The aggressive, overt activities of Satan and demons are to be much more pronounced as the end times close in upon us.

> But woe to the earth and the sea,
> because the devil has gone down to you!
> He is filled with fury,
> because he knows that his time is short.
> (Revelation 12:12)

A third reason for increased awareness of the battle is that sin abounds in our day. The more wicked man becomes, the more open and obvious the power of Satan will be displayed. This is particularly true of sins that involve occultism and sexual licentiousness. A society that is deeply characterized by pornography, licentiousness, drugs, alcoholism, sorcery, witchcraft, and open Satan worship is a society that will see much open and obvious activity of demons.

What are believers to do in preparing themselves to meet the challenge? This book encourages believers to use warfare prayer and other practical means to reach certain victory. Believers must personally avoid and diligently guard their families from any involvement in occult practices. Ouija boards, party seances, levitation, transcendental meditation, tarot cards, horoscopes, and the like should be totally avoided. Indulging curiosity about such things is like walking unarmed into the enemy's territory.

> When you enter the land the Lord your God is giving you, do not learn to imitate the detestable ways of the nations there. Let no one be found among you who sacrifices his son or daughter in the fire, who practices divination or sorcery, interprets omens, engages in witchcraft, or casts spells, or who is a medium or spiritist or who consults the dead. Anyone who does these things is detestable to the Lord, and because of these detestable practices the Lord your God will drive out those nations before you. You must be blameless before the Lord your God. (Deuteronomy 18:9-13)

We must also take care that we do not develop an excessive curiosity about Satan's workings. Books and films that describe the practices and orgies of witches' covens and Satan worship are out of place for believers. On the pretext of becoming informed, some well-meaning people are doing a dangerous disservice to the Christian community. Knowing the details of the rites and rituals of witchcraft is harmful and totally unnecessary. Most of us would readily see harm in a Christian's reading pornography or viewing pornographic films to better understand that area of sin, but we may fail to see harm in curiosity about witchcraft and Satanism.

We must also guard against being fearfully preoccupied with Satan and his activities, thus giving him undue prominence. Hope and courage are vital words in spiritual warfare. Courage is not only necessary in facing our relentless foe, but it is also the believer's purchased possession. Satan would like nothing better than to fill believers with dread of him and his kingdom. If he can keep his work shrouded in an aura of mystery or if he can cloak his programs with sensationalized hocus-pocus in the minds of believers, Satan will have accomplished one of his chief aims.

"Be self-controlled and alert. Your enemy the devil prowls around like a roaring lion looking for someone to devour. Resist him, standing firm in the faith" (1 Peter 5:8-9*a*). Satan roars to make us afraid and thus more vulnerable, but our purchased right is courage to resist him.

Fear is one of the most prevalent reasons believers may not get involved in spiritual warfare. They hope that by ignoring the subject they will avoid having to face their enemy directly. Some say to me, "How involved do I need to become in spiritual warfare when I'm not aware of any particular problem?" My response is always to remind them that they already *are* involved if they are believers. Whether we want to be or not, Satan presses the battle to us in close, relentless encounter. Ephesians 6:12 declares that ours is a wrestling battle, a close, hand-to-hand struggle with Satan's highly organized kingdom. To those who appreciate the awesome power of Satan's kingdom, this personal struggle is a fearsome prospect. Yet the underlying thesis of Ephesians 6 is that every believer has the certainty of victory: ". . . and after you have done everything, to stand" (Ephesians 6:13).

Prayer is the means by which we aggressively claim our strength in the Lord, appropriating the power of the Holy Spirit and putting on the whole armor of God. There is no substitute for a prayer life that brings the truth of God's Word into aggressive application. That is what Peter touched on when he told us to resist the devil, "standing firm in the faith." "The faith" is the whole body of God's truth, the absolute, eternal verities of doctrine that cannot be broken.

How courageous should believers become in applying their victory against Satan? Some evangelical Christians have resorted to exorcism of wicked spirits, even from the lives of other believers. Some cases have brought encouraging results, but at other times the benefit of that practice has been very questionable.

A story from the *Chicago Tribune* of March 27, 1975, carried this disturbing headline: "British Wife-Killer Stirs Exorcism Debate." The article reported that three hours after a man went through a seven-hour "ancient ritual of exorcism," he killed and mutilated his wife. A canon of the Church of England was quoted as saying, "The . . . meddlers will dabble about in demonism not knowing what they are doing or what might happen. The damage it can do is immeasurable." Edward Rogers, head of social responsibility for the Methodist Church, added a more moderate but equally careful word: "Carefully administered, exorcism could act as a form of psychological help, but badly done, it can be a form of psychological disaster."[1]

Similar news accounts of the practice of exorcism of demons are common and equally controversial. What ought to be the attitude of believers toward the practice of boldly confronting demonic powers? The Lord Jesus and His disciples did on many occasions confront wicked spirits and boldly demand that they reveal their presence (Mark 5:9; Acts 16). As believers united with the Lord Jesus Christ in

1. *The Chicago Tribune,* 27 March 1975.

all of His person, position, and victory, we do have authority over all wicked powers (Ephesians 1:21; 2:6; 6:10-18), and there may be occasions on which a bold confronting of the enemy is necessary. The hour in which we live may force this work upon us. I sought to touch on some of those occasions and procedures in chapter 9 of *The Adversary.*

But I believe far greater emphasis should be upon the troubled believer's consistent warfare praying, the use of sound doctrine in his daily walk, and the practice of separated, godly living. Individual believers must know how to exercise their authority over Satan and demons in a commanding way.

Believers must see anew their privilege and responsibility of walking victoriously as men and women of God. No believer who willfully walks in the sins of the flesh and the world can hope to escape Satan's hurt and bondage (Galatians 5:13-26; 1 John 2:15-17). Can you imagine what would happen to a soldier who took a little stroll into his enemy's territory during the heat of war? If not killed, he would soon be surrounded and taken captive. Yet there are believers who think they can carelessly engage in sin without being vulnerable to Satan. Ephesians 4:27 warns, "And do not give the devil a foothold." That's what he is looking for—a foothold to get in the door of the believer's life. He seeks to hurt, bind, and destroy us through our worldliness or other sin. Unless we know our way to victory, we become vulnerable.

Victory over fleshly sin comes first by honestly admitting our old nature's capacity to be sinful. That's why lists like Galatians 5:19-21 are given to us. God isn't surprised by our old nature. He knows its wickedness, and He wants us to know it too. The second step in overcoming fleshly sin is to count ourselves dead to the old nature (Romans 6:5-6; Galatians 5:24). With Christ the "old man" is put to death. The third step is to walk in the Spirit and ask Him to put within our inner lives the fruit of His fullness (Galatians 5:22-23). He will do so as we yield to the truth of His inspired Word. Moment-by-moment application of our victory works wonders in defeating sins of the flesh.

Victory over the flesh, the world, and the devil is all provided for us. Appropriating that victory and walking in it is our responsibility. Willfully doing otherwise will lead to disaster and may require a fierce battle with Satan before freedom returns.

I believe that one of the greatest needs for the church is that believers be aware of the seriousness of our battle against Satan and the practical, spiritual help that brings us victory. Such victory must be part of our daily spiritual walk. This book will help believers in victorious warfare living and prayer.

1

Satan Is Not Invincible

For eight wonderful months we were privileged to have in our home a lovely young lady, twenty-two years of age, who had been a heroin addict for at least five years. Before coming to us, Sandy had been detoxified in a prison hospital. She began to thrive in the secure environment of our Christian home. She was like a flower beginning to unfold. In her freedom from drugs, she began to see a whole new world around her, and she realized what she had missed during her bondage. She enjoyed going to church. She even made a profession of faith to receive Jesus Christ as her Savior. Her job as a nurse's aide in a local convalescent hospital became a delight as she comforted and helped the elderly patients. Her gift as a talented pianist began to return. Everything looked bright and encouraging.

All went well until one of her old friends found out where she was. He invited her to attend his sister's wedding with him. Reluctantly, at her insistence, we let her go. She later told us that on that very night she had started back on the road to drugs. Although we loved her very much, it wasn't long until we had to tell her that she would either have to live under the disciplines of our family, or she would have to leave.

The night she chose to leave we talked about her profession of faith. With unusual insight she pointed to her head and said, "I have it up here, Pastor B., but I never meant it down here," pointing to her heart. What a dark night it was for us as we watched her drive away in the new car her father was helping her purchase. Satan seemed so powerful in that moment, and we seemed so weak. A few months later I conducted her funeral. She had died of an overdose. Whether it was self-administered or forced, no one knows. Satan is indeed very powerful.

Christ's Powerful Love

However, there is a brighter side to this story. During the months after Sandy left, our family never ceased to pray for her. We had frequent calls and contact with her, sometimes to help her out of a tight spot. Always she told us she loved us.

One August day, the phone rang in my office. It was our oldest daughter, Rhonda, who was visiting from out of state. She told me that Sandy was at the parsonage, wanting to see me. I dropped everything and hurried home.

I wasn't prepared for what I saw. Sandy had just walked away without release from a local hospital where she was being treated for an overdose. Her beautiful long black hair had been hacked off just below her ears by an angry boyfriend. Her face was an emaciated facsimile of the once beautiful girl who had been in our home. She was suffering not only from the overdose but from a liver ailment. Her clothing was dirty and torn. I took her in my arms and began to cry. My demonstration of love seemed to break her heart, and she sobbed and sobbed out her hurt on my shoulder.

When we were able to talk, I said to her, "Sandy, you know you are soon going to die, living this way, don't you?" She looked at me a moment, and again her eyes filled with tears as she nodded. We talked about her admission that her previous profession of faith had only been a head assent and not a heart belief. We looked at numerous Bible passages showing that eternal hope comes only to those who come heart-first to the Lord. She must of her own will acknowledge her sin and repent. She must really want to be free from the power of sin and drugs and believe that the Lord Jesus Christ could save her from all of her sins.

A terrible battle was being waged. Satan's hold upon her was being threatened, and he was fighting fiercely. At times she would seem to harden and even laugh. At other times she seemed almost to blank out. During those moments I would stop and pray aloud for her. "In the name of the Lord Jesus Christ, I bind away Satan's interference with Sandy's coming to know the Lord Jesus Christ. I invite the Holy Spirit to convict Sandy of her need of being saved from her sins. Lord Jesus Christ, open her eyes to see how much You love her."

I kept assuring Sandy that no one could make that decision for her. She had to invite Christ personally to enter her life and heart and save her soul. I had determined not to make it easy for her. I did not offer to help her pray the sinner's prayer as I had done at the time of her previous profession. I told her it had to come from her heart. She needed to pour out her heart in repentance toward God and invite the

Lord Jesus to enter her life and cleanse all of her sins away.

The struggle went on for some time. One moment she seemed near deciding for Christ, the next moment she wanted to put it off until another time. Finally, I prayed a doctrinal prayer over her, claiming Christ's finished work against Satan and pleading our Lord's gracious love for Sandy.

The moment of victory came. Without any further prompting on my part, Sandy was on her knees praying. Out of her deepest soul poured forth words of sorrow for her sins and love for Christ like I have seldom heard. She expressed her longing for the Lord Jesus Christ to enter her life and free her from her sins. The tears were flowing freely, not only from her eyes but from mine as well. When she had finished her prayer, I began to pray again that the Lord would free her from all of Satan's bondage and from any demonic powers that had laid claim to her life.

Sandy was kneeling in the middle of our living room floor with her face buried in her hands on the carpet. As I prayed for her release, she began to cough profusely and to retch as though vomiting out some invisible poison. The powers of darkness that had laid such deep claim to her life for so long were leaving. It was as if wave after wave had to leave, and each time the coughing and retching would painfully convulse her body. Sandy didn't seem to really understand what was happening, but she knew it was good. I kept praying for the Lord to clean all powers of darkness out of her life and to free Sandy completely.

When Sandy finally sat up, a radiant smile lighted her whole countenance. She looked beautiful and peaceful. The shine of heaven was radiating through all the scars of sin.

"I can't believe it," she said, "I've never felt so clean inside. I'm really saved. Jesus Christ really does love me. I can't believe it. It really has happened to me." Yes, Satan is powerful, but he is not all powerful. His terrible hold on a human life had been broken again.

As I look back upon that day, I feel I made a serious misjudgment at that point. Sandy wanted to go to her parents and tell them what had happened, and we let her go. She told her parents of her decision and said, "Mom and Dad, you need never worry about me again. Even if I die tonight, I know I'm going to be in heaven."

What happened after that we do not fully know. She told her father that she was going to turn in some "very bad" people to the authorities. He was convinced that those "very bad" people could not cope with that new girl and gave her a forced drug overdose. No one really knows, but our one joy is that we have no doubt that Sandy is absent from her body and "at home with the Lord." Satan is powerful, but he is not invincible. Warfare prayer had brought one of life's most desperate wreckages through for Christ. The funeral service was a time of expressed victory. I shared the testimony of her conversion with the large gathering of her family and friends. Many of them did not know Christ and were deeply moved by the service.

Underestimating the Enemy

Every time Satan appears in Scripture, there is an aura of unusual power surrounding this fallen created being. The Bible seems to indicate that God has never created any other being as powerful as Satan. Even Michael the archangel, one of the holy angels of God, was apparently no match for Satan in one direct encounter (see Jude 9). Michael had to appeal to the Lord to rebuke Satan. Satan's awesome power is further seen in the gospel accounts of the temptation of Jesus. No one can read of that encounter in the wilderness without developing a sober respect for the power and position of this archenemy of God and His kingdom. Yet, there is urgent necessity to know that Satan is not invincible. He is always "second best." He is a mere creature, no match for the Creator!

At times the battle may grow fierce, and we may feel that Satan is winning. Daniel must have felt that way when he was praying for twenty-one days for an answer to an urgent prayer of his heart (Daniel 10). He tells us that during that time he was in a state of mourning. As an expression of his deep faith toward God, he was going through a limited fast and other practices of self-denial.

Daniel's prayer had reached heaven the very first day, but the answer was delayed by a powerful prince of the kingdom of Persia, who had stood in the way of the holy angel's coming with God's answer to Daniel. Only as Daniel continued to pray and fast after those twenty-one days was the holy angel able to come (see Daniel 10:1-15). What if Daniel had thought Satan too powerful for him to gain an answer to this request? Perhaps the angelic messenger would not have come.

Do we give up too soon and miss the answers to our prayers? Christ may someday reveal the answer to that question, but the challenge of it ought to move us to pray with more faithful tenacity. Satan is not invincible, but we can be and ought to be. It is the Lord's will that we be provided all we need to do the Lord's will.

Satan's Tactics

How deceitful Satan is when he tries to convince us that he is too powerful for us. One young professional man called me about his battle with Satan's kingdom. He was an athlete and very strong, both physically and intellectually. Yet, he had been plagued by ceaseless harassment from demonic powers. They afflicted him with annoying physical sensations and at times controlled his tongue so that he hissed like a snake. When those things happened he seemed unable to help himself.

I pointed out to him the principles of warfare as best I could by telephone and sent him other material. For a time those things seemed to help, but then his affliction seemed to grow worse. Recently he called me again. As he related his battle to me over the phone, he conveyed a message of despair and hopelessness. I could understand that in light of his long battle, but I knew he had to be shocked out of his despair.

After letting him talk on about his battle and defeats for some time, I said, "I guess Satan really is stronger than God after all. He has you, and you might as well give up because there is no hope."

The response was instantaneous and gratifying. He saw what I was trying to say. "That's what I'm really saying, isn't it?" he replied. "I've fallen into the trap of convincing myself that I'm defeated. Pastor, pray for me." We joined in prayer over the telephone. While I was praying, the powers of darkness tried to take over, but we continued to pray and rejoice in our invincible position of victory in Christ. Their power was broken. He was able to praise the Lord for the battle and even the defeats he suffered, rejoicing in the Lord's purpose for the prolonged battle.

A woman called and related her difficult struggle in spiritual warfare. As I tried to share with her the principles of aggressive spiritual warfare, she responded by assuring me that she'd done all of that for many years. She insisted that her situation was unique and difficult beyond what anyone else had experienced. She would need some very special attention before she could ever hope to be free, because Satan had such a strong hold upon her life. The secret of the enemy's strength in her life was this: She was assigning to him an invincible role in her life that he was only too happy to assume.

Once we do that we are locked into a cycle of defeat. We can't win because we know we can't. Such a person looks for someone to help him who isn't subject to Satan's "invincible" strength as he is, but even his Christian friends are helpless until the lie the person believes is renounced. Satan is not invincible. He is a defeated foe. Any apparent victory he has in our lives is only temporary. "We are more than conquerors through him [Christ] who loved us" (Romans 8:37).

Satan wants us to worship him. He took the Lord Jesus to a high mountain and showed Him "all the kingdoms of the world and their splendor. 'All this I will give you,' he said, 'if you will bow down and worship me' " (Matthew 4:8-9). If he would dare to try to get the sinless Son of God to worship him, he will employ his most subtle tricks to try to get those who belong to Christ to do the same.

Oh, very seldom will he be so brash as to try to get you to actually kneel and worship—at least not at first. He is much more subtle. He will just try to get you to exalt his power in your own thinking to the point where you regard yourself as his helpless ploy. At that point, so far as you are concerned, he is indeed an invincible foe. When you fall into that trap, you are ascribing to Satan an honor that is a kind of worship—a worship composed of fear and subjection.

When I was a young man, my father would sometimes have three or more purebred bulls as part of his herd. It was inevitable that one of those bulls would have to prove in battle with the others that he was "in charge." Once that had been proved, the defeated ones would always give him the right to rule and would not challenge his authority again. That illustrates what Satan tries to do with us. When he defeats us once or several times, he is simply seeking to establish his right to rule. He wants believers to accept the fact that he is stronger than they are and that he is "in charge." Once we accept that fallacy, he has us caught in a psychological defeat that does not belong in the Christian life.

Misled by Experience

There are times experience seems to defy truth. A lady from Canada claimed to have used faithfully the principles of warfare set forth in *The Adversary.* "I've done it all," she said, "but it just doesn't work for me. I've prayed doctrinal prayers, I've read and memorized the Word, I've aggressively and consistently resisted the devil and his demons, but I'm still harassed constantly." She was discouraged, defeated, and desperately looking for some quick relief. She lamented that there didn't seem to be anyone near who was interested in helping her. Her experience of battle was a direct challenge to the truth of God. She was so defeated that she was not even attending church.

As we talked, I asked her if she had ever thanked her Lord for the battle. I asked her if she had ever prayed that the Lord would teach her everything He wanted her to learn through this prolonged battle. She confessed that she had not. Her attitude had been that this battle with Satan's kingdom was all bad and that the only thing God would want for her would be immediate and total victory. When she saw that God might want to teach her stability and faithfulness in spite of the battle and in the very midst of the greatest defeat, it opened up an entire new vista for her.

We talked about her neglect of church attendance and fellowship with the body of believers as an admission to Satan of his victory. Her "giving up" on warfare praying and saying warfare principles were "not working" were admissions that Satan was winning. She needed to stand upon the truth and not let the experience of her battle remove her from it.

That is what the apostle Paul keeps emphasizing in his great doctrinal exhortations of Romans 5 and 6. We must stand upon truth and not allow subjective experience to challenge the absolute of truth. Only as we do that will the subjective experience begin to harmonize with truth. Subjective experience is never to be trusted as a valid establisher of spiritual truth. The revealed Word of God establishes truth.

In Romans 6:5-10 the apostle Paul expounds the truth that each believer is united with Christ in His total victory over sin and death and Satan. That is an infallible truth upon which each believer is responsible to stand. Sin and Satan cannot rule over a dead person. Sin cannot master and put into slavery a person who is now "alive unto God" because of our union with Christ in His resurrection. That is infallible, unchanging truth upon which we are meant to stand regardless of experience.

Satan will ceaselessly seek to challenge the truth. He will bring all the harrassment he can muster into your experience to make you think that for you this just doesn't work. He keeps saying by your experience that sin is too strong and he can and will reign in your life.

What is Paul's answer to such attack? "In the same way, count yourselves dead to sin but alive to God in Christ Jesus. Therefore, do not let sin reign in your mortal body so that you obey its evil desires" (Romans 6:11-12). Paul's challenge is repeatedly communicated in similar doctrinal passages. We must stand upon truth. Our responsibility is to affirm as fact that we are "dead" to the rule and reign of sin, of death, and of Satan in our lives.

We are "alive to God." Our Lord is ruling. Our responsibility is to "not let sin reign." Sin and Satan can reign only if we "let" him do so. We "let" him reign when we accept the fact that "it doesn't work" or we neglect "assembling together" because the experience of battle is too great. The moment we allow Satan an invincible role in our lives because of our experience of battle and our experience of defeat, we are letting him reign. Victory comes because we have certainty of our victory through our Lord Jesus Christ.

There is no point at which the believer needs to "cave in" and admit defeat at the hands of Satan's craft and power. There is hope and victory available for the most defeated. The church at Laodicea illustrates this point. That body of believers had succumbed to Satan's deception. Spiritual lukewarmness had taken over. That church felt itself very sufficient and spiritually victorious. They were saying: "I am rich; I have acquired wealth and do not need a thing." They were so blinded by Satan's clever deception that they didn't know they were "wretched, pitiful, poor, blind and naked" (Revelation 3:17). Yet, even to people so totally deceived, the Lord Jesus offered full access to His victory.

> "I counsel you to buy from me gold refined in the fire, so you can become rich; and white clothes to wear, so you can cover your shameful nakedness; and salve to put upon your eyes, so you can see.
>
> "Those whom I love I rebuke and discipline. So be earnest, and repent. Here I am! I stand at the door and knock. If anyone hears my voice and opens the door, I will come in and eat with him, and he with me." (Revelation 3:18-20)

That great offer and assurance belongs to every believer. No matter how far Satan has come in deceiving and controlling us, we can have gold tried in the fires of refining; white, clean garments; and salve of healing to remove our spiritual blindness. Close, intimate, in-the-heart fellowship with Christ is there to be claimed. Satan is not invincible, but Christ is, and the believer is invincible in Him.

Prayer of Victory

Loving heavenly Father, I praise You that Satan is a defeated foe. I rejoice that his defeat was accomplished by the Lord Jesus Christ in His sinless life, His death, burial, resurrection, and ascension into glory. I look forward to that day when the Lord Jesus Christ rules, while Satan is bound in the bottomless pit. I know that Satan will ultimately be forever consigned to the lake of fire prepared for him and his angels. I rejoice that You have given to me, in my union with the Lord Jesus Christ, complete victory over Satan today.

I enter into my victory aggressively and claim my place as more than a conqueror through Him that loved me. I refuse to admit continuing defeat by Satan in any area of my life. He cannot and will not rule over me. I am dead with Christ to his rule. I affirm that the grace and mercy of God rule in all areas of my life through my union with the Lord Jesus Christ. Grant to me the grace to affirm Your victory even when experiences of life seem to say otherwise.

I thank You for these battles and all that You are seeking to accomplish in Your wisdom and design for my life. I accept the battle and rejoice in Your purpose. I willingly accept and desire to profit from all of Your purpose in letting Satan's kingdom get at me. I reject all of Satan's purpose. Through the victory of my Lord and Savior I stand resolute and strong upon the certainty of my victory. In confidence I look to You, Lord Jesus Christ. When Your purpose for this trial is fulfilled, I know that it shall fade into the dimness of forgotten battles and a defeated enemy. Through the precious name of the Lord Jesus Christ, it shall be so. Amen.

2

Keeping a Sovereign Perspective

Above everything else, Christians need to cultivate a faith that establishes them as winners. This is all-important. Anything less gives Satan and his kingdom a devastating advantage.

Coach Bear Bryant in his lifetime became a football legend. Above all, he is remembered as a winner. At the end of his thirty-eight-season career he held six national championships and more victories than any other coach in college football history.

Victor Gold, in a tribute to Bryant's career, writes of him in the February 19, 1983, issue of *National Review:* "Like all authentic Southern legends, he was of the soil. 'If I hadn't found football,' he once said, 'I'd have ended up behind a mule, just like my daddy. But I'll tell you one thing. I'd have plowed the straightest furrow in Arkansas.' "[1]

Somebody once asked him, "Don't you consider yourself an innovator? A stylesetter?"

"No," he said, "I ain't nothin' but a winner." The winning career and philosophy of life espoused by Bear Bryant says something important to believers. We need to know that through grace and redemption's victory we are nothing but winners.

Habakkuk lived in a day much like our own. Moral and spiritual degeneracy, expressed in violence and injustice, were everywhere he looked. In his prayers he cried, "How long, O Lord, must I call for help, but you do not listen? Or cry out to you, 'Violence!' but you do not save? Why do you make me look at injustice? Why do you tolerate wrong? Destruction and violence are before me; there is strife and conflict abounds" (Habakkuk 1:2-3).

A prophet in our day might have the same lament when viewing the

1. © 1983 by National Review, Inc., 150 East 35 St., New York, NY 10016. Reprinted with permission.

contemporary world scene. Satan's program is a cacophony of violence, injustice, and brutality. Promising much, Satan always delivers little. The more he exerts his sway, the more frightening and chaotic matters become in individual lives and in society as well. Satan is a usurper. He tries to hold power by force without any right to do so. That is why it is important to know our biblical, or legal, ground of authority when under attack by Satan's kingdom.

Your Legal Rights

Some dear friends of ours went through some very dark days. Seizures, much like those of an epileptic, would come upon the wife, particularly at night, with no apparent medical explanation. Doctors believed the seizures were from some sort of anxiety attack, but they had never seen it manifested in that way. Psychologists explained that the attacks were from repressed anger. Our friends revealed the problem to me as we discussed spiritual insights into their trying time.

There seemed reason to suspect demonic causes for the seizures, but it is best to be cautious in such delicate emotional situations. Hasty and simplified answers can be not only unfair but also very harmful. Yet by observation and experience, I had come to know that such attacks *could* certainly be demonic in origin. Satan is a clever intensifier of human weakness. He desires to push to the ultimate any problem that originates in human weakness. Psychological problems we might otherwise work through rather easily can almost destroy us when intensified by Satan.

We discussed the possibility of Satan's involvement. Not only were the seizures painful, but they were frightening as well. We carefully considered the believer's biblical authority to refuse Satan the right to rule any area of our lives. In Romans 6 they saw their privilege and responsibility to "not let sin reign in your mortal body so that you obey its evil desires" (Romans 6:12).

A careful procedure was planned. The next time a seizure began, they were immediately to challenge any of Satan's involvement by forbidding him to rule in this way. We talked of how the husband could come to his wife's rescue by challenging any spirit of darkness behind the seizure. He was to say, "In the name of the Lord Jesus Christ and by the power of His blood, I resist any spirit of darkness that is trying to cause my wife to have a seizure. I forbid you to do it. I command you to leave our presence and to go where the Lord Jesus Christ sends you." He was urged to insist repeatedly until the seizure was broken. His wife was encouraged as best she was able to repeat the challenge her husband addressed against Satan.

As our friends utilized this strategy, the seizures ceased completely. In this case demons had indeed been involved and were seeking to intensify a human weakness.

Our subtle enemy will do anything to try to deceive us into his control. If he can convince us that our problems are not of his doing, he can continue his work. Blaming the devil for all our troubles is never wise, but neither is dismissing his involvement too quickly.

Let's use an illustration to demonstrate how important it is to know your biblical rights when challenging Satan's usurping efforts. Suppose one day you answer the door and there stands a powerfully built man who boldly pushes his way into your house before you can object. His towering size and forceful voice overwhelm you. He makes himself right at home and takes over. You try to find out why he is there, but he is evasive, saying he is your friend and just wants to be neighborly.

The man of the house tires of the intrusion and suggests that the family would appreciate his leaving so that they can have dinner. "Oh," says the big man, "that's a great idea. When do we eat?"

Baffled by this brash intrusion but respecting the strong man's size, the head of the house hesitates to throw the intruder out. Dinner is served, and the big fellow eats most of it. After dinner he proceeds into the living room and monopolizes the conversation. The family grows increasingly uncomfortable, but the man's size, his piercing eyes, and his powerful voice intimidate everyone.

Dad finally suggests that it is getting late and that perhaps the man should leave because it is time to go to bed. The big man laughs and says that he is tired too; he has decided to stay and sleep in the main bedroom. By this time everyone is exasperated, but what can be done? One sweep of his powerful hand would wipe them all out. He just goes into the bedroom and takes over. He is too big to throw out. Intimidated, they are forced to let him stay.

By now, the illustration is becoming ludicrous. How unthinkable that any of us would let that happen. Big or not, the man has to go. He's an intruder, a usurper. He has no right to enter, let alone stay. What can we do to get rid of him?

If we are wise, we will call the police and force him to leave. He may be too big for us to handle, but all the authority of the law and government are on our side. If it takes a whole militia to do the job, justice and authority will not allow him to stay. Yet we must initiate the action. Our requests don't get him to leave. Threats only make him laugh because of his strength and size. We are impotent against his strength. He would stay forever if we fail to appeal to legal authority.

Satan is that kind of foe. He is much more subtle, but that is very descriptive of how he operates against Christians. Ephesians 4:27 warns us not to give the devil a foothold. He pushes his way into our lives, where he has no legal right to be. He will try to convince us that our weakness, demonstrated by our sins and failures, gives him that right. Once we have opened the door by giving in to a particular sin, he insists that he will stay around as long as he desires. Intimidated by his power and guilt-ridden by our sins, we fearfully conclude that maybe he does have the right after all.

We are not talking about a Christian's being possessed by Satan. The apostle Paul was certainly not possessed by Satan, but he was able to experience deep affliction and some sort of demonic oppression that greatly troubled him.

> Even if I should choose to boast, I would not be a fool, because I would be speaking the truth. But I refrain, so no one will think more of me than is warranted by what I do or say. To keep me from becoming conceited because of these surpassingly great revelations, there was given me a thorn in my flesh, a messenger of Satan, to torment me. Three times I pleaded with the Lord to take it away from me. But he said to me, "My grace is sufficient for you, for my power is made perfect in weakness." Therefore I will boast all the more gladly about my weaknesses, so that Christ's power may rest on me. (2 Corinthians 12:6-9)

There are two important lessons to be drawn from Paul's experience. Of first importance is to always challenge Satan's intrusions into our lives.

Paul knew that Satan had no *legal* right to be a distracting influence in his life. He had every right to "resist the devil" with the certainty that Satan would have to "flee from him." He had all authority, every legal right, to insist that this demonically caused affliction leave him. All the authority of his union with Christ in the Savior's Person and finished work belonged to Paul. Satan had no "legal claim" on Paul. Neither does he have any legal claim on other believers. That is the very heart of the message of the finished work of Christ. Hebrews 2:14-15 sums it up for us: "Since the children have flesh and blood, he too shared in their humanity so that by his death he might destroy him who holds the power of death—that is, the devil—and free those who all their lives were held in slavery by their fear of death." The Lord Jesus Christ's work frees us legally and completely from Satans claims.

There is yet another important lesson to learn from Paul's experience. We must allow our Lord to be sovereign. For Paul to insist upon his "legal" rights in his case would have been an insult to his Lord. In

His sovereignty, the Lord had a purpose in allowing Satan to afflict the apostle. This illustrates a vital principle of spiritual warfare. In our battle, our Lord must always be kept first in importance. Even in direct battle with Satan, our primary dealings are with God. He has a purpose in our struggle with the forces of darkness that is for our good and His glory.

That fact is never more clear than in the Old Testament account of Job. All of Job's troubles, pain, and torment were satanically caused. Yet, Job kept all of his attention centered upon his Lord as he worked through his horrendous trials.

Job knew a very important principle about a righteous man's dealings with the devil. He knew that his Lord had a sovereign purpose in the struggle. It was the same awareness that Paul recognized, accepted, and delighted in. When we are battling with Satan and the powers of darkness two important dimensions need to be kept in view. First, we must know that because we are united with Christ we have full authority to resist Satan and to force him to leave our presence. Yet at the same moment we must be willing to accept our Lord's sovereign purpose for allowing us to experience the battle, even if it is prolonged.

I often urge those facing an intense struggle with Satan to say two things. The first expresses positive, faith toward the Lord: "In the name of the Lord Jesus Christ, I accept every purpose my Lord has for allowing me to experience this fierce battle with Satan. I desire to profit and to learn all of my Lord's purpose in this battle." The second is negative, rejection of Satan's purpose: "In the name of the Lord Jesus Christ and by the power of His blood I reject every purpose of Satan and his kingdom in afflicting me in this battle. I command every wicked spirit behind this affliction to leave my presence and to go where the Lord Jesus Christ sends him."

Sometimes when we are under affliction from the enemy our only thought is to have the experience end. How many times people have called me wanting to know a quick formula for instant deliverance. It is painfully difficult but eminently necessary for those suffering such affliction to remember to keep the Lord's sovereignty in view. Sometimes it is the Lord's plan to set people free immediately, but at other times the prolonged battle may be in His sovereign plan. Yielding to our Lord is always paramount in spiritual matters. It is His will that needs to be done and not our own. It is often in life's most painful experiences that we grow the most.

Though I have lost the source, I recall reading a story that was related by Festo Kivengere, the renowned Anglican Bishop of Uganda.

During the Ugandan rule of the dictator Idi Amin, many Ugandans were killed for the slightest offense—real or imagined—against the government. Many of those killed were Ugandan Christians.

As one believer was being fastened to a tree for execution by a firing squad, he asked to be allowed to speak to his tormentors. Looking directly into their eyes and with a strong voice, he declared, "I love you, and I love my country! As I die, I would like to sing to you." He smiled, and the words of his song flowed out with calm assurance: "Out of my bondage, sorrow and night, Jesus, I come; Jesus I come." While he was singing that hymn, the shots rang out and he died, but he died an invincible Christian. He was "more than a conqueror." He was nothing but a winner.

While pastoring in southern California, I received a heart-breaking report of a tragic accident involving some very dear friends of ours. Tim and I had served together as neighboring pastors in another state for nearly twelve years. We had grown very close, serving in the same denomination, sharing joys and burdens. We were prayer partners. It was a shock to learn of the accident. A drunk driver had veered across the dividing line and crashed head on into the small car Tim had been driving. His wife was instantly killed, and Tim was in very critical condition.

I could feel Tim's sorrow and pain. As I made my way to the intensive care unit of the hospital, I wondered what I would say. What could I communicate that would minister to one grieving and crushed by such sorrow and physical hurt? Tim and his wife had been so close. Theirs was a bright example of Christian marriage at its best.

Walking toward Tim's bed, I noted the extensive life-support equipment. The attending nurse related the seriousness of Tim's condition and asked me to make my visit brief. Tears filled my eyes as Tim's eyes met mine. Trying to control my emotions, I took his one uninjured hand in mine and just held it a moment. "Tim," I finally was able to say, "I'm so sorry. I love you very much." Though he couldn't speak with his voice, his eyes and countenance spoke eloquently. That sparkle of faith and smile of confidence I had known so well still greeted me. Something radiated from within him. It was like a shining fire. I had come to comfort Tim with a few Scripture promises, a word of love, and a prayer of support. Yet in that moment the ministry of the Holy Spirit flowed from his life to minister to me. He was moving through that tragedy as "more than a conqueror." He was experiencing what it is to be invincible. I left knowing that he would recover and that his life would continue to manifest the strength of God's invincible people. He too was nothing but a winner.

The apostle Paul climaxes his epistle to the Ephesians by setting forth four keys to strength that enable believers to always remain winners. No matter how fierce the battle becomes, no matter how much pressure Satan brings to bear, no matter that to human perspective it seems otherwise, we will remain triumphant as we utilize what God has provided.

Four Keys to Victory over Satan

The four keys are: (1) the believer's union with Christ, (2) the Person of the Holy Spirit, (3) the whole armor of God, and (4) the allness of prayer. We shall look at each of these more in detail in subsequent chapters, but it seems vital to establish them early in our thinking.

"Finally, be strong in the Lord" (Ephesians 6:10*a*). Our strength and assurance of victory center on our being "in the Lord." Our inseparable bond to all of His person and work assures us of being nothing but winners. "Finally, be strong . . . in his mighty power" (Ephesians 6:10*b*). Just as the first phrase speaks of the entire Person and work of the Lord Jesus Christ, so the second phrase speaks of the Person and work of the Holy Spirit. The final words of the Lord Jesus Christ to His disciples focused on the origin of power in the life of a believer. "But you will receive power when the Holy Spirit comes on you" (Acts 1:8). It is through the Holy Spirit that we experience "the power of His might." We shall need to understand how to appropriate the Person and work of the Holy Spirit in our warfare.

The third key is the supplying of the whole armor of God for both protection and projection.

"Put on the whole armor of God so that you can take your stand against the devil's schemes" (Ephesians 6:11). Each part of the armor has a unique and strategic part to play in the securing and maintenance of the believer's victory. Victorious believers will maintain a growing appreciation of the armor throughout their lifetimes. We must acquaint ourselves with our armor.

The fourth key carries an importance all its own because it remains the means by which a believer appropriates the other three. "And pray in the Spirit on all occasions with all kinds of prayers and requests. With this in mind, be alert and always keep on praying for all the saints" (Ephesians 6:18). I know of no way to appropriate one's union with Christ apart from using prayer. The Person and work of the Holy Spirit in our daily lives are as related to prayer as air is related to breathing. The Holy Spirit does not intrude His dominion and power into our lives. He waits to be invited to demonstrate His mighty power through us. The practice of prayer is absolutely essential to putting on one's armor. We will study more fully the use of prayer and its essential role in insuring that as believers we remain winners.

Centered on God

Loving heavenly Father, enable me to keep all things within the perspective of Your sovereignty. Grant to me the wisdom to know that the fierceness of the battle is not evidence of defeat. Help me to thank and praise You for Your purpose in each phase of the battle. I reject all of Satan's purpose for his attack upon me, but I accept all of Your sovereign plan and purpose. I thank You for what You are doing by allowing Satan's kingdom to war against me. Use the battle to refine, to deepen, to mature, to humble, and to build my faith.

Grant to me the insight and understanding to know my victory. I desire that the roots of my assurance of victory would go down deeply into the essential doctrines of Your Word. I want to see myself as being invincibly strong through my union with Christ, the Person and work of the Holy Spirit, the wholeness of Your provided armor, and the allness of prayer. Teach me how to appropriate my victory in a practical, daily practice. These things I ask in the name of my Lord Jesus Christ. Amen.

3

The Believer's Union with Christ

> Finally, be strong in the Lord and in his mighty power. (Ephesians 6:10)

That is an order issued by a trained captain of warfare, the apostle Paul, a strong word given by the Holy Spirit to Christian soldiers, who are facing a powerful enemy. What a command that is! The use of the Greek imperative makes it a command we are to obey. The theological implications are obvious. We are meant to be invincible in our warfare. We should settle for nothing less.

In Romans 8, after revealing the lofty position of the believer—he has been predestined, called, justified, and glorified—Paul dramatically declares the invincible strength of the believer in warfare. "What, then, shall we say in response to this? If God is for us, who can be against us?" (Romans 8:31). The answer he expects from us is a shout of victory. "Absolutely no one!" Not even Satan himself can successfully be against believers who know their ground of victory. A few verses later Paul restates that assurance of victory: "No, in all these things we are more than conquerors through him who loved us. For I am convinced that neither death nor life, neither angels nor demons, neither the present nor the future, nor any powers, neither height nor depth, nor anything else in all creation, will be able to separate us from the love of God that is in Christ Jesus our Lord" (Romans 8:37-39).

No wonder this man who knew the strength that belonged to him could say, "I can do everything through him who gives me strength" (Philippians 4:13). He knew he was invincible in battle. Everything standing in the way of God's will for his life had to move aside—Satan, demons, and any other power.

Knowing we are spiritually invincible in fulfulling God's will for our lives is a necessary prerequisite to effective warfare praying. Satan is a very successful liar. He spares no subtle tactic to try to intimidate believers and to convince them that they are weak. Satan wants us to think that we are defenseless in light of his awesome power. Unless we know the biblical basis of our invincible position, he will doubtlessly succeed in convincing us that we are no match for his assaults.

Some months back, a man came to me who was having a severe battle with the powers of darkness. They had been tormenting him for many years in numerous ways. He often had horrible dreams full of sadistic violence or vile sexual orgy. During his waking hours, he heard cruel voices that urged him to do hideous acts that revolted his sensitive Christian spirit. At other times, he experienced physical pain that seemed to be caused by the powers of darkness. Psychiatric care and counseling had not been able to relieve his torment.

As I counseled with him, I sought to lead him to aggressively resist the assaults on the ground of his own spiritual authority as a Christian. The believer must fearlessly and aggressively resist the attack using an approach of this type:

"In the name of the Lord Jesus Christ, I come against the power of darkness causing these voices to suggest these hideous acts to me. *[Be sure to name whatever symptom you are experiencing.]* I come against you in the power of my union with the Lord Jesus Christ, and through His precious blood I resist you. I bind your whole kingdom to you. *[Wicked spirits are structured much like a military organization with leaders and others who follow the leader's orders.]* I bind you from working, and I command you and your kingdom to leave me and to go where the Lord Jesus Christ sends you."

When I first suggested this approach to the man, his response was, "Oh, I would be afraid to do that. Satan might overwhelm me. I'm not very strong spiritually, and I don't think I would dare to ever speak against Satan like that."

That is a classic example of how Satan gets us to believe his lies. This man had an inadequate concept of his biblical position. He didn't know his true authority. He did not see his position as being strong and invincible. Through study of the Word and patient encouragement, he was eventually able to begin to claim his victory. When he did, the problem immediately began to cease.

It is important that our vision of being invincible rests upon the solid truth of the Word of God. Our authority must have biblical foundation. Presumptuous courage that originates in some wrong belief will not only lose many battles, but it is also very dangerous. The battle we face is not small. When we talk about being invincible and able to defeat Satan's kingdom, we must not let such knowledge cause us to become careless. Our invincibility over Satan's kingdom does not mean that his power amounts to not much after all. We must always remember that Satan's power is second only to the power of God Himself. Jude 8 and 9 warn us never to treat lightly the power of our enemy. "In the very same way, these dreamers pollute their own bodies, reject authority and slander celestial beings. But even the archangel Michael, when he was disputing with the devil about the body of Moses, did not dare to bring a slanderous accusation against him, but said, 'The Lord rebuke you!' " (Jude 8-9).

The seven sons of Sceva, a Jewish chief priest, learned that lesson in a painful way. While Paul was at Ephesus, these usurpers tried to use Paul's formula without knowing the truth behind it. As they tried to deal with wicked spirits, they said, "In the name of Jesus, whom Paul preaches, I command you to come out" (Acts 19:13). The results they got were very painful: "The evil spirit answered them, 'Jesus I know and Paul I know about, but who are you?' Then the man who had the evil spirit jumped on them and overpowered them all. He gave them such a beating that they ran out of the house naked and bleeding" (Acts 19:15-16).

Courage in Christ

The believer needs courage. He must not be fearful; yet, he must be sure that his courage is resting upon that which really makes him invincible. Ephesians 6:10 says, "Be strong in the Lord." That little phrase *in the Lord* is one of the most important we will ever come to understand. It is the very cornerstone to our knowing that we are invincible in spiritual warfare.

The phrases *in the Lord, in Christ,* or their equivalent appear over forty times in the book of Ephesians alone. Such repetition lets us know that it is not just a convenient cliché. Every Christian is inseparably united with the Lord Jesus Christ. We are placed by God into oneness with His Person and work. Christ's work belongs to every believer by right of intimate union. Second Corinthians 5:17 states concisely and decisively: "Therefore, if anyone is in Christ, he is a new creation; the old has gone, the new has come!" Being "in Christ" is a doctrinal fact, an absolute truth that grants to the believer a new stance. The old bondage and fear of Satan has been broken. All of Christ's victory has become ours.

What does it mean to be "in Christ"? What is there about this relationship that makes us invincibly strong? How can we use this truth in warfare prayer? How can it make our resistance to Satan victorious?

First, being "in Christ" means that we are in the mighty victory of the *name* of the Lord Jesus Christ. What a great source of power for victory His name represents. Philippians 2:9-11 conveys to us something of the power we have by being in His name:

> Therefore God exalted him to the highest place
> and gave him the name that is above every name,
> that at the name of Jesus every knee should bow,
> in heaven, and on earth, and under the earth,
> and every tongue confess that Jesus Christ is Lord,
> to the glory of God the Father.

His is a name "above every name"— that speaks of a place of security and invincible strength. "Every knee shall bow" in submission to the power of that name. Satan himself and all of his kingdom are included.

It is important daily to pray the security and strength of His name over your personal life, your family, and the call of God upon your life. It is in the name of the Lord Jesus Christ that we are strong and invincible.

To be "in Christ" also means we are united to Christ in all of the victory that He achieved in His redemptive work. At the moment of conversion, God puts the believer into all the victory Christ achieved in *His incarnation.* One of the most astounding truths about the redemptive work of Christ is that in the Person of Christ, God Himself became a human being. The humanity of Christ remains one of the great wonders of eternity. It was in His incarnate form, as one of us, that our Lord Jesus Christ achieved our redemption and totally defeated the kingdom of darkness (Hebrews 2:14-15).

First John 4:2-3 states: "This is how you can recognize the Spirit of God: Every spirit that acknowledges that Jesus Christ has come in the flesh is from God, but every spirit that does not acknowledge Jesus is not from God. This is the spirit of the antichrist, which you have heard is coming and even now is already in the world."

The truth concerning God's entering the world in the Person of Christ, the truth that God was in Christ, that God Himself became a human being is a great defeat, a devastating threat to Satan's kingdom. John tells us that is a truth so threatening and devastating to the kingdom of darkness that fallen beings will not freely admit that Jesus Christ has come in human flesh.

Victory over Satan belongs to us through our union with Christ in His incarnation. It is experienced by those who appropriate and use that mighty truth against our enemy. Can you not see how defeating it is to your adversary if you focus the truth of your union with Christ in His incarnation against Satan and his kingdom? Our hope for the daily favor and blessing of God upon us while we yet live on this earth is uniquely related to the truth that we are included in the perfect worthiness of Christ in His humanity. He always lived a human life that was worthy of God's best blessings. Though tempted in every way, He remained without sin. He was always in fellowship with the heavenly Father, always utterly holy and worthy of God's best. As we walk in this world, His worthy human life belongs to us. It is ours. God sees us in Him. We do not expect those manifold blessings of God day by day because of how good and successful *we* are in living a perfect life. No, we expect His blessings because our incarnate Savior lived a perfectly worthy life, and we are "in Christ."

To be "in Christ" also means that we are in the work and victory won by *His death.* The sufferings and the death of our Lord Jesus Christ are equally vital to our invincible position of victory in warfare praying. "Since the children have flesh and blood, he too shared in their humanity so that by his death he might destroy him who holds the power of death—that is, the devil—and free those who all their lives were held in slavery by their fear of death" (Hebrews 2:14-15).

In redemption's plan, God puts believers into the death of Christ with all of its victory over our enemies. It remains for us to aggressively lay hold of our union with Christ in His death and apply it as a part of our responsibility in invincible warfare. This is conveyed to us in passages like Romans 6:11-12, "In the same way, count yourselves dead to sin but alive to God in Christ Jesus. Therefore do not let sin reign in your mortal body so that you obey its evil desires." The fact that we are commanded not to let sin reign in our mortal bodies is evidence that even believers can have this problem. If believers do not appropriate and apply their union with Christ in His death, sin in its various expressions will rule. We are responsible to "count," to affirm as truth the fact that we are dead to sin's reign. We are united with Christ in His death. Because of that doctrinal fact we are dead to the rule of sin but alive to God's reign.

The cross and the blood of our Savior are a great threat to Satan's kingdom. In the cross, Jesus Christ brought Satan's kingdom to nothing. As believers aggressively apply the death of Christ, claiming all of its benefits to their personal lives, to their families, and to their ministry for the Lord, they too become invincible with Christ in His death. "And having disarmed the powers and authorities, he made a public spectacle of them, triumphing over them by the cross" (Colossians 2:15).

To be "in Christ" suggests further victory in that it means we are in His resurrection. The same mighty power that raised up our Lord Jesus Christ from the grave belongs to us and is ours. No wonder that long after he had become a believer, Paul would write to the Philippians and say, "I want to know Christ and the power of his resurrection and the fellowship of sharing in his sufferings, becoming like him in his death, and so, somehow, to attain to the resurrection from the dead" (Philippians 3:10-11). Being "in the Lord" means that mighty power of the resurrection is ours to be known and used to make us invincible in our warfare.

To be "in Christ" has further application to our being seated with Christ in the heavenlies. "And God raised us up with Christ and seated us with him in heavenly realms in Christ Jesus" (Ephesians 2:6). After His resurrection, the Lord Jesus Christ was

> seated . . . at his right hand in the heavenly realms, far above all rule and authority, power and dominion, and every title that can be given, not only in the present age but also in the one to come. And God placed all things under his feet and appointed him to be head over everything for the church, which is his body, the fullness of him who fills everything in every way. (Ephesians 1:20-23)

The ascension of Christ into glory was the sealing moment of His finished triumph, a portrayal of His supreme victory "far above all rule and authority." Being seated with Christ there, our "in Christ" position is a truth demonstrating our "in the Lord" authority to resist the devil and to defeat him. We are united with Christ in all His ascended authority and power.

One final thought needs to be stressed. To be strong, invincible "in the Lord," means we know and apply the truth that we are united with Christ in His watchful *headship* over His church. He is our great High Priest and the glorified Shepherd of His sheep. How beautiful it is to be able to know that we are united to our living Savior, who is building His church; to know that He has said, " 'Never will I leave you; never will I forsake you.' So we say with confidence, 'The Lord is my helper; I will not be afraid' " (Hebrews 13:5-6).

There is much in those little phrases *in Christ* and *in the Lord* to help us know that it is God's will we be invincibly strong. Satan's roaring never need frighten us if we are "in Christ."

A woman shared with me a fascinating story that illustrates the nature of our invincible warfare when aggressively applied.

In her youth she had attended a fine Bible college, where she gained a good foundation of biblical knowledge. In later years as she reared her family, she admitted that her faith became more of a practice of habit than a vital life of day by day walking with Christ. Though an active participant in a Bible preaching church, she lacked a warm consistent relationship with her Lord. She became an "institutional"

Christian. Such professional Christianity can often lead to disaster, as it did in her case.

Her relationship with her husband left much to be desired. Her three teenage children were headed for disaster. Her oldest son was hopelessly caught in the drug scene and was drifting without any goals. Her teenage daughter was involved in a flirtatious affair with a married man and refused to be warned against the dangers and tragedies of her course of life. Her youngest son, yet in high school, was headed the same way as his older brother. This Christian mother was desperate and didn't know what she could do to remedy the tragedy of her life and that of her family.

She called me one day to tell me that she had read *The Adversary.* The challenge to practice doctrinal praying as set forth in that book had moved her heart. She began to focus such prayer upon her home and children. Five months later she was calling to share with me the results.

Her oldest son had renounced his involvement with drugs and was making plans to enter a Bible college. Her daughter had ended the relationship with the married man and was nearing engagement with a dedicated Christian. Her youngest son had renewed his commitment to Christ and was taking an active part in the leadership of his youth group at church. Joyfully she shared other dramatic spiritual results that God was bringing into her life and home. Although doctrinal praying is not always that dramatic in producing change, I relate this account as a very obvious testimony to the practical benefits of a vision to be invincible in warfare prayer. Focusing the victory of Christ upon our personal lives, upon our families, and upon our unique area of ministry will always reap significant rewards. Before I bring this chapter to a close, I want to share a prayer that focuses on our "in Christ" relationship.

Claiming Our Union

Loving heavenly Father, I praise Your name. I've come to see that it is Your will that I be invincibly strong in my spiritual warfare. I praise You, Lord, that You have placed me "in Christ." By faith I express my desire to abide in the protection and blessing of the mighty name of the Lord Jesus Christ. I pray the omnipotent power of His name over my family and the ministry to which You have called me. I pray the name of the Lord Jesus Christ against Satan and all that his kingdom would do to hinder God's plan for my life.

I focus my prayer on my union with Christ in His incarnation. I joyfully confess that Jesus Christ has come in human flesh to win my victory for me. I pray all of the triumphs the Lord Jesus achieved in His humanity against all of Satan's subtle wiles and crafty deceits. I pray the victories of the incarnation over all areas of my life and ministry.

I praise You for the cross and death of the Lord Jesus Christ, desiring all the benefits of His death to focus upon my life, my family, and my ministry. I affirm that my death with Christ can defeat the control and rule of sin, of death, and of Satan. I desire the shed blood of Christ to be against all that Satan is doing to hinder me.

I hunger to learn more deeply what it means to experience the power of His resurrection. Just as I desire to be dead to the reign of sin, so I long to live in accord with the fact that I am alive unto God through the power of the resurrection. In the mighty power that raised up the Lord Jesus Christ from the dead, enable me to walk in the newness of life available to me.

Heavenly Father, it will always remain a marvel to me that You have seated me with Christ in the heavenly realm, far above all principalities and powers. Humbly I use the authority of my ascended union with Christ to pull down all of Satan's plans formed against me personally, all of his plans formed against my family, and all of his plans formed against God's appointed plan for my life.

Thank You, Lord Jesus Christ, that in Your glorified position at the Father's right hand, You are leading Your church and shepherding Your sheep. I deliberately submit to Your lordship of my life and ministry. I acknowledge that everything that is good about my life, home, and ministry is because of Your lordship and gracious blessing.

By faith I claim my invincible right to be strong and victorious in Your complete salvation. I refuse to be discouraged. I reject all emotions that make me feel defeated. I choose to live as one who is more than a conqueror through Jesus Christ my Lord. In the name of my Lord Jesus Christ, I pray with thanksgiving. Amen.

4

The Person of the Holy Spirit and His Mighty Power

> Be very careful, then, how you live—not as unwise but as wise, making the most of every opportunity, because the days are evil. Therefore do not be foolish, but understand what the Lord's will is. Do not get drunk on wine, which leads to debauchery. Instead, be filled with the Spirit. Speak to one another with psalms, hymns and spiritual songs. Sing and make music in your heart to the Lord, always giving thanks to God the Father for everything, in the name of our Lord Jesus Christ. (Ephesians 5:15-20)

> Finally, be strong . . . in his mighty power. (Ephesians 6:10)

Several biographers of D. L. Moody relate an account of what became a significant turning point in his effective ministry for God. Moody had been preaching for several years. He was in great demand as a speaker. He was the founder and leader of one of the fastest growing and most effective Sunday schools in Chicago. His ministry attracted even the attention and curiosity of Abraham Lincoln, who insisted on visiting Mr. Moody's Sunday school on one of his visits to Chicago. Moody's influence and ministry were reaching out farther and farther, but he had an area of weakness that needed recognition.

Following one of Mr. Moody's evangelistic meetings, two ladies lingered behind to speak to him. "We have been praying for you," they said, implying that they saw a need for prayer in his life and ministry.

That bold statement disturbed Moody. "Why don't you pray for the people?" he asked rather abruptly.

"Because you need the power of the Holy Spirit," they responded.

Ruffled, Moody responded, *"I* need the power?"

But those two ladies took the assignment from the Lord to pray that Mr. Moody be endued with the Holy Spirit's power. They were frequently in the front rows of his meetings, obviously much in prayer. At first Mr. Moody responded with annoyance, but his sincere heart soon began to respond in a positive way. Before long, the cry of his own heart was to be endued with power. He would frequently gather a group for a half day of prayer. He would "groan and weep before God" for the Spirit's enduement.

Then something unique happened in a hotel room in New York City. The authorized biography of Moody by William Moody, his son, quotes the evangelist as saying:

> "I was crying all the time that God would fill me with His Spirit. Well, one day, in the city of New York—oh, what a day!—I cannot describe it, I seldom refer to it; it is almost too sacred an experience to name: Paul had an experience of which he never spoke for fourteen years.
>
> I can only say that God revealed Himself to me, and I had such an experience of His love that I had to ask Him to stay His hand. I went to preaching again. The sermons were not different. I did not present any new truths, and yet hundreds were converted. I would not now be placed back where I was before that blessed experience if you should give me all the world—it would be as the small dust of the balance."[1]

Another biographer states, "God seems to have answered in a mighty way the prayers of these two women, for at this time his life changed considerably from that of a young, somewhat cocky and proud preacher, to a humble, soft and mellow-hearted preacher, who quietly, but richly, revealed . . . the compelling teaching of God's great love for men everywhere, as it is revealed in the Bible."[2]

Giving the Person and work of the Holy Spirit place in his life effected profound changes in Mr. Moody's ministry. He found new power and effectiveness in snatching people from Satan's bondage. Walter Knight writes of the subsequent effectiveness of one of Moody's meetings in London. He preached to 5,000 people, many of whom were professed atheists, agnostics, and free-thinkers. Unbelief was so much in vogue in that day that special clubs were organized all over London to foster fellowship among those who had rejected the faith. They came to Moody's meeting with cynical minds and scornful looks. Moody was tempted to be intimidated by these learned, scornful skeptics, but instead he claimed the mighty power of the Holy Spirit. He preached the Word of God with great fervency and conviction.

1. William R. Moody, *Life of D. L. Moody* (Kilmarnock, Scotland: John Ritchie, n.d.), 66.
2. Harry J. Albus, *A Treasury of Dwight L. Moody* (Grand Rapids: Eerdmans, 1949), 35.

Knight quotes Moody's own evaluation of the results:

> In an instant, the Holy Spirit moved upon those enemies of Jesus Christ. More than five-hundred of them stood. Tearfully they cried out, "I will! I will come to Christ!" Quickly the meeting was closed for personal work to begin. From that night until the end of the week nearly two thousand men were won from the ranks of Satan into the army of the Lord. The enduring character of what took place was evidenced by the discontinuance of their atheistic clubs![3]

D. L. Moody became one of Christendom's most powerful proponents of the necessity of the Person and work of the Holy Spirit in believers' lives. He knew how dramatic could be one's victory over sin and Satan when filled with the Spirit's mighty power. He carefully avoided the excesses that have sometimes characterized emphasis upon the Holy Spirit's ministry. Yet, Mr. Moody was always ready to proclaim the truth that believers must be filled with the Spirit. The thousands upon thousands won to Christ during his evangelistic preaching resulted from the Spirit's empowerment. The revival meetings that sometimes went on for weeks with Mr. Moody preaching nightly also witness of that power.

Being filled with the Holy Spirit's power remains at the heart of all spiritual victory and Christian service. The great importance the Scripture assigns to the doctrine of the Holy Spirit is doubtless the reason there is so much confusion among believers about this subject. Both rational intellectualism and excessive emotionalism have tended to rob Christians of the marvelous ministry of the Holy Spirit in their lives. The kingdom of darkness is doing all that it can to keep the Holy Spirit's Person and work shut away from our practical usage.

The Danger of Seeking Spiritistic Manifestations

On the one hand Christians face the problem of excessive emotionalism surrounding the Person of the Holy Spirit. This emphasis too often stresses experience and spiritistic manifestations into which demonic powers are always ready to intrude. Dr. Merrill Unger in his book *What Demons Can Do to Saints* has documented several such cases. One illustration came to him from the wife of a Baptist minister in Kansas. She wrote him describing her salvation at the age of ten, telling of the terrible bondage to demon powers under which she had fallen. The following is her own account:

3. Walter B. Knight, *Knight's Illustrations for Today* (Chicago: Moody Press, 1970), 150.

Many times during the next twenty years a great hunger came to my soul to know the Lord better. Not being a student of the Word, I did not really understand the simplicity of God's teaching to be filled with the Spirit and walk in the Spirit.

In 1967 a friend gave me a book about speaking in tongues. My spiritual life was at a low ebb, and I was intensely seeking after God. I knew I was saved, but there seemed to be an emptiness in my soul.

After reading this book, I began to believe that the experience of tongues was necessary to fill the spiritual void. For six years I asked for the experience.

During 1973 I became ill. The desire for a closer fellowship with the Lord and to have the power of God upon my life became more intense than ever before. I read several books on tongues . . . and I began seeking out people who had this experience.

My husband, a Baptist minister and a student of the Word, would explain the Scripture teaching on this subject, but my mind was made up that tongues were the ultimate and only reliable evidence of being Spirit-filled.

I contacted a charismatic Baptist minister and received the laying on of hands, which brought a most ecstatic experience . . . undoubtedly supernatural. I had never experienced such a wonderful feeling—too different to be merely psychological. I felt certain no one had ever been so happy, contented, and filled with joy.

Tongues did not come to me with the laying on of hands, but I kept asking for them. Two months later they came, accompanied with unusual happenings.

Each day was a new and wonderful experience. Prayers were answered, miraculously, and always in the name of Jesus. One of the greatest deceits is the "other Jesus spirits," who do not confess Jesus Christ as Savior and Lord (1 Jn 4:2; 2 Co 11:4).

At that time no one could have made me believe that Satan could produce these happenings, although the Word of God warns that he is "prince of the power of the air" (Eph 2:2).

The week that tongues came to me, strange happenings occurred inside my body. My will had no control over the happenings, and I was doing nothing to produce them.

Some of the manifestations were lewd and my mind was greatly disturbed, since they always came after the tongues, which I supposed were produced by the Holy Spirit.

The tongues were new and exciting, and I used them frequently at first. I knew the physical happenings were demonic, but I thought Satan was trying to defeat the wonderful experience of the Holy Spirit.

I was filled with glory over the tongues, but at the same time, suffered agony over the constant evil that prevailed. I returned to my charismatic friends time after time for help. Each time there was the laying on of hands and the command for Satan to leave me alone.

Although the physical manifestations never left me, for several days I would have relief from the mental oppression.

I asked for more tongues, going deeper into the experience, trying to get away from Satan. When the glory of the "high" was over after each tongues experience, the presence of evil was more prominent.

Many times it seemed the entire room was filled with evil.

Several months after receiving the tongues experience and alternating from day to day between glory and misery, a still, small voice spoke definitely to me, saying that the tongues were a form of Satan worship. Being certain that this was the work of the Holy Spirit, I was horrified, although the suspicion had existed for some time.

Being increasingly certain that I was being controlled by Satan, I determined to resist him. Torment beyond description followed. Voices would speak to me about the most hideous things imaginable.

Horrible suspicions about my husband and dear Christian friends took hold of me. Terrifying dreams and nightmares occurred. Voices said that I should die because I was corrupt, and God would never use me now.

Sometimes becoming desperate with fear of losing my sanity and life, I would yield to the tongues which were welling up within me. Great relief followed, until I refused them expression again.

Many times I called upon the Lord and claimed the blood of Christ. But each time I would be thrown to the floor in agony. Fourteen months after receiving the tongues, I was ready to take my life.

As a final plea for help, I called a very dear Baptist minister-friend, who knew something of these Satanic workings among God's people. He worked and prayed with my husband and me about three months. Other ministers prayed with us, sometimes for several hours at a time.

During this time we saw the power of the resurrected Christ demonstrated against the foe in a spectacular way.

Although I had lent myself through ignorance to the influence of the evil powers of Satan, the Lord in love continued to draw me out of the snare of the enemy.

It has been a long journey back from the realm of darkness into which I had gone so deeply, but the grace of the Lord Jesus Christ has been sufficient to meet every need.

This is not a conviction or accusation of others who speak with tongues. I am only testifying of what is true in my personal experience as a result of my mind having been corrupted from the simplicity that is in Christ (2 Co 11:3).

I have many friends and loved ones in the Pentecostal-Charismatic movement whose desire is to serve the Lord Jesus Christ. Many of them preach the true Gospel of Salvation. Some of these became very dear to me during the times of great stress and had a sincere desire to help and encourage me.[4]

4. Merrill F. Unger, *What Demons Can Do to Saints* (Chicago: Moody Press, 1977), 81-84.

That account expresses one side of the danger. There is another side as well. Dead, cold, unbiblical intellectualism concerning the Person and work of the Holy Spirit gives Satan equal advantage against us. So called "institutional Christianity" has come under criticism in recent years. When religious worship is reduced to lifeless, impersonal ceremony, it is no wonder that people look elsewhere for their joys of life. Satan's program looks very appealing in contrast to the drab institutionalism that often makes up modern worship.

A Balanced Perspective of the Spirit's Filling

Nearly all the serious errors that have divided and hindered the Christian church have somehow been related to a lack of balance. There are many apparently paradoxical truths in Scripture that require balanced understanding. The sovereignty of God and the free will of man are a case in point. Predestination and the doctrine of election are thrilling doctrinal truths. Yet, if we ignore the Bible's teaching on man's opportunity for choice and responsibility for decision, we will inevitably get into trouble. The Word of God puts equal emphasis on both teachings.

Balance is the key to recognizing the work of the Holy Spirit in effecting victory. The Holy Spirit's ministry toward believers as set forth in God's Word has at least seven aspects. Balance is required to keep those ministries in proper perspective. Excessive emphasis upon one of the Spirit's ministries at the expense of the others begins to destroy balance. The enemy gets us preoccupied with tangents that rob our time and distract from the whole. As we daily appropriate the Holy Spirit's power, it is helpful to keep in mind the Spirit's seven unique ministries.

THE SPIRIT'S CONVICTING MINISTRY

> But I tell you the truth: It is for your good that I am going away. Unless I go away, the Counselor will not come to you; but if I go, I will send him to you. When he comes, he will prove the world wrong about sin and righteousness and judgment: about sin, because men do not believe in me; about righteousness, because I am going to the Father, where you can see me no longer; and about judgment, because the prince of this world now stands condemned. (John 16:7-11)

The convicting ministry of the Holy Spirit has its primary expression before we come to know Jesus Christ as our Lord and Savior. The Lord Jesus told the grumbling Jews in John 6:44, "No one can come to me unless the Father who sent me draws him, and I will raise him up at the last day." The heavenly Father draws us by His Holy Spirit, convicting us of our sin, of God's righteousness, and of the certainty of judgment to come. Though I was only eight when converted to Christ, the convicting work of the Holy Spirit is still vivid in my memory. I knew I was sinful and needed to be saved. On the day of Pentecost, after the Holy Spirit came and Peter had preached his sermon, the conviction of the Holy Spirit was present in power. "When the people heard this, they were cut to the heart and said to Peter and the other apostles, 'Brothers, what shall we do?' " (Acts 2:37).

The Holy Spirit takes God's Word and applies it to human hearts. Guilt for sin, the righteousness of God, and accountability deserving judgment are brought to the human heart by the Holy Spirit. That is how unbelievers come to know Christ as Lord and Savior. This ministry of the Spirit is going on constantly in our world.

There is a sense in which the Holy Spirit also brings conviction upon believers if they have unconfessed sin in their lives. It is a different kind of conviction, however. It comes as the wooing, loving appeal of our heavenly Father to His children. It does not center upon judgment and wrath but rather upon broken fellowship and the need for restored relationship (see 1 John 1 and Hebrews 12:1-15).

Unfortunately, much so-called conviction in the lives of believers is really false guilt that is thrust upon them by the "accuser of the brethren." Revelation 12 anticipates that day when "the accuser of our brothers, who accuses them before our God day and night, has been hurled down. They overcame him by the blood of the Lamb and by the word of their testimony; they did not love their lives so much as to shrink from death" (Revelation 12:10-11).

We must understand the work of Satan's kingdom, or we may tragically attribute to the Holy Spirit what is really Satan's doing. Few believers escape Satan's clever ways of heaping guilt and self-condemnation upon themselves. He and his workers try to destroy a believer's sense of self worth with accusations. "Look at you," comes the taunt. "You claim to be a Christian, yet you feel hate toward God and His Word. What kind of Christian are you? You deserve to be judged and go to hell." Such thoughts should be recognized as Satan's work. The Holy Spirit does not deal with believers that way. He may well point out acts of disobedience to us, but only to help us see the forgiveness and cleansing available through the blood of Christ. His purpose is to restore and assure us of God's love, forgiveness, and renewed fellowship.

One cannot warn too strongly of the importance of discerning the difference between the Holy Spirit's loving work toward believers and Satan's accusing, destroying actions. Consider the following comparisons:

The Holy Spirit's Work	Satan's Work
1. Seeks to show you that your infinite worth and value to God make Him desire your fellowship.	1. Seeks to convince you that you are so bad God wouldn't want to have anything to do with you.
2. Seeks to show you that there is forgiveness and restoration available no matter how bad your sin.	2. Seeks to convince you that there is no forgiveness for you. You've committed the unpardonable sin.
3. Uses God's Word to give you hope and assurance of God's love and forgiveness.	3. Uses God's Word out of context to convince you that there is no hope for you.
4. Builds faith, hope, and love in your heart and increases your confidence and assurance of salvation.	4. Creates despair, doubt, resentment, and anger toward God, His Word, and His people. You feel that no one as bad as you could ever really be saved.

False guilt is one of the most common maladies affecting believers today. Freedom from such guilt is exciting and liberating. "You'll never know, pastor, what a life-transforming thing it has been to me to be free of false guilt. Ever since I was saved I've been haunted by my awareness of the sinful desires of my old nature. I'd feel so guilty and condemned when these desires would come to me. Now I see that these desires are just the expression of what God said my old sin nature is like. I am now able to reject them, and I seldom feel that destroying, paralyzing, self-condemning guilt anymore. If I do, I know how to fight it." A Christian engineer shared this testimony with me recently. It's the kind of testimony the Holy Spirit wants to give to every believer.

THE SPIRIT'S INDWELLING MINISTRY

"You, however, are controlled not by your sinful nature but by the Spirit, if *the Spirit of God lives in you.* And if anyone does not have the Spirit of Christ, he does not belong to Christ" (Romans 8:9, italics added).

That text makes clear that the Holy Spirit comes to dwell within a believer at the moment of his salvation. John 3:6 states, "Flesh gives birth to flesh, but the Spirit gives birth to spirit." The Holy Spirit at the moment of one's new birth comes to dwell within the spirit of the believer. He is a literal presence, a dwelling within the believer's body. "Do you not know that your body is a temple of the Holy Spirit, who is in you, whom you have received from God?" (1 Corinthians 6:19-20).

Understanding that truth should protect us from some of the excesses of today's religious scene. We do not need more of the Holy

Spirit. We have Him living, dwelling within our very beings. It remains for us to recognize His presence and to welcome His Person and work within us. We do not need more of Him; He needs more of us. We are to yield daily to His Person and His work within us. D. L. Moody's desire was not for the Holy Spirit but for His power, His anointing for service. We will study that more as we consider the filling ministry of the Holy Spirit.

Recognizing and appropriating the Holy Spirit's indwelling presence has much to do with our success as Christians. Because He dwells within us, we can ask Him to daily produce within us the fruit of the Spirit. "But the fruit of the Spirit is love, joy, peace, patience, kindness, goodness, faithfulness, gentleness and self-control. Against such things there is no law" (Galatians 5:22-23). The producing of that fruit does not require some new, super experience with the Holy Spirit. It is a matter of faith practiced on a daily basis. As the old nature tries to rule by causing us to mainfest some of its expressions as set forth in Galatians 5:19-21, it is our responsibility to affirm that we are dead to its rule and then ask the Holy Spirit to produce His fruitful work within us.

The indwelling of the Holy Spirit is also the reason we can expect to understand God's Word as we read it and study it. However, as it is written:

> "No eye has seen,
> no ear has heard,
> no mind has conceived
> what God has prepared for those who love him"—
> but God has revealed it to us by his Spirit.
>
> The Spirit searches all things, even the deep things of God. For who among men knows the thoughts of a man except the man's spirit within him? In the same way no one knows the thoughts of God except the Spirit of God. We have not received the spirit of the world but the Spirit who is from God, that we may understand what God has freely given us. (1 Corinthians 2:9-12)

That aspect of the Holy Spirit toward believers is often called His illuminating work. As we depend upon the indwelling Spirit of God when we study the Bible, He will bring its truth into our understanding. That is why it is so important to ask the Holy Spirit to illumine God's truth as we study or memorize it.

Many benefits flow from the indwelling work of the Holy Spirit. He is able to sanctify us, to keep us growing in grace, to give us His peace, and to enable us to practice love. Through His indwelling presence, He distributes the spiritual gifts He wants each believer to have (Romans 12:1-8; 1 Corinthians 12; Ephesians 4:7-13).

THE SPIRIT'S BAPTIZING MINISTRY

> The body is a unit, though it is made up of many parts; and though all its parts are many, they form one body. So it is with Christ. For we were all baptized by one Spirit into one body—whether Jews or Greeks, slave or free—and we were all given one Spirit to drink. (1 Corinthians 12:12-13)

The baptism "in the Holy Spirit," or "with the Holy Spirit," or "by the Holy Spirit" is a doctrine often disagreed upon by various ecclesiastical groups. Some insist that this work comes after salvation and is accompanied by speaking in tongues. 1 Corinthians 12:13 describes baptism by the Spirit as a work of the Holy Spirit that places all believers into Christ's body. His body is described in Ephesians 5:22-23 as His church. The Holy Spirit baptizes every believer at the moment of his conversion into the Body of Christ, the body of all true believers. Just as a profession of faith and water baptism seem to have been the two requirements for entrance into the *local church* of the New Testament, so the new birth, accompanied by Holy Spirit baptism, is the means by which God puts us into the Body of Christ. Though our conversion may well be accompanied by joyful feelings, the baptism by the Spirit does not necessitate some experiential "high." Like justification, it takes place apart from experience. It's a marvelous comfort to realize that I do not need to seek and groan and strive to be baptized by the Holy Spirit. That work of the Holy Spirit unites us to the Lord Jesus Christ and to other believers as soon we believe.

THE SPIRIT'S SEALING MINISTRY

> And you also were included in Christ when you heard the word of truth, the gospel of your salvation. In him, when you believed, you were marked with a seal, the promised Holy Spirit, who is a deposit guaranteeing our inheritance until the redemption of those who are God's possession—to the praise of his glory. (Ephesians 1:13-14)
>
> And do not grieve the Holy Spirit of God, with whom you were sealed for the day of redemption. (Ephesians 4:30)
>
> Now it is God who makes both us and you stand firm in Christ. He anointed us, set his seal of ownership on us, and put his Spirit in our hearts as a deposit, guaranteeing what is to come. (2 Corinthians 1:21-22)

Those texts make clear that sealing is a work of God, apart from any effort or striving on our part. We are sealed unto God the moment we are saved.

The sealing work of the Holy Spirit guarantees your security and assurance of eternal life. Satan and his kingdom will ceaselessly challenge your assurance of salvation. He will assert that you are not good enough to make it to heaven. What indescribable comfort and ceaseless praise should come to us in knowing that the seal of ownership is God's doing. It is the Holy Spirit who seals us until the day of redemption, guaranteeing what is to come. The believer's security centers in the complete Trinity. The Father holds us in His grasp: "My Father, who has given them to me, is greater than all; no one can snatch them out of my Father's hand" (John 10:29); the Son secures us: "My sheep listen to my voice; I know them, and they follow me. I give them eternal life, and they shall never perish; no one can snatch them out of my hand" (John 10:27-28); and the Holy Spirit seals every believer (Ephesians 1:13; 4:30).

In my view, the security of the believer is one of the most important biblical doctrines. If we have an understanding of our security hidden deeply in our faith, not even Satan himself can convince us to doubt.

THE SPIRIT'S QUICKENING MINISTRY

> And if the Spirit of him who raised Jesus from the dead is living in you, he who raised Christ from the dead will also give life to your mortal bodies through his Spirit, who lives in you. (Romans 8:11)
>
> But because of his great love for us, God, who is rich in mercy, made us alive [quickened] with Christ even when we were dead in transgressions—it is by grace you have been saved. (Ephesians 2:4-5)

Quickening means bringing the dead to life. The Holy Spirit does that for believers. "As for you, you were dead in your transgressions and sins, in which you used to live when you followed the ways of this world and of the ruler of the kingdom of the air, the spirit who is now at work in those who are disobedient" (Ephesians 2:1-2). This text makes clear that before God brought us to spiritual life through the quickening work of the Holy Spirit, the ruler of the kingdom of the air, Satan, had a terrible hold upon us. After the Holy Spirit brought spiritual life into us as believers, we were set free from Satan's rule.

The quickening work of the Holy Spirit has three phases to it. We were quickened and brought to spiritual life by the Holy Spirit the day we first believed. We are being quickened as we daily walk in the Spirit and experience His life-giving work (Galatians 6:16-26). We will yet be quickened at the Lord's coming when the Holy Spirit accomplishes that glorifying work in our mortal bodies (Romans 8:11; see also 1 Corinthians 15:42-58; Philippians 3:21; 1 Thessalonians 4:13-18).

Our bodies need the quickening power of the Holy Spirit before they will be ready to enter the glory of heaven. In Romans 6, the apostle Paul calls the body "the body of sin." "For we know that our old self was crucified with him so that the *body of sin* might be rendered powerless, that we should no longer be slaves to sin—because anyone who has died has been freed from sin" (Romans 6:6-7, italics added). Verses like this seem to indicate that the old nature still has the potential to rule over us through our human bodies that have not yet been quickened and glorified. The body is in process of dying; death is upon it, but it will one day be quickened in resurrection power by the Holy Spirit. We will then have glorified, never-dying bodies like the one Jesus Christ had when He arose from the grave. "But our citizenship is in heaven. And we eagerly await a Savior from there, the Lord Jesus Christ, who, by the power that enables him to bring everything under his control, will transform our lowly bodies so that they will be like his glorious body" (Philippians 3:20-21).

THE SPIRIT'S INTERCEDING MINISTRY

> In the same way, the Spirit helps us in our weakness. We do not know how we ought to pray, but the Spirit himself intercedes for us with groans that words cannot express. And he who searches our hearts knows the mind of the Spirit, because the Spirit intercedes for the saints in accordance with God's will. (Romans 8:26-27)
>
> And pray in the Spirit on all occasions with all kinds of prayers and requests. With this in mind, be alert and always keep on praying for all the saints. (Ephesians 6:18)
>
> But you, dear friends, build yourselves up in your most holy faith and pray in the Holy Spirit. (Jude 1:20)

Those texts remind us that we have help with our praying. The Holy Spirit enables us to "pray in the Holy Spirit." That means that He comes to our side and helps us frame our prayers. It also means that He prays for us when we may be completely silent but depending upon the Holy Spirit to bring our requests before the throne of grace with His deep groanings.

Surely every believer has experienced the frailty of humanity that is common to us all, a frailty that may make prayer difficult. Sometimes as we wait on the Holy Spirit, He will free our minds and lips to express our longings to God. At other times, we may just kneel before the Lord in silence knowing that the Holy Spirit is bringing our petitions before God.

To say that "praying in the Spirit" requires the use of an unknown tongue is not correct. Paul makes clear in 1 Corinthians 14:13-17 that praying in the Spirit includes the use of the mind. Paul's prayers for the Ephesians (Ephesians 1:15-22; 3:14-19) and the believers in Colosse and Philippi were prayers in the Spirit. To pray in the Spirit simply means that we are being enabled by the Holy Spirit's control to pray according to His Word and His will. He enables us to pray and intercede in ways that we could not without His help.

THE SPIRIT'S FILLING MINISTRY

> After they prayed, the place where they were meeting was shaken. And they were all filled with the Holy Spirit and spoke the word of God boldly. (Acts 4:31)
>
> Therefore do not be foolish, but understand what the Lord's will is. Do not get drunk on wine, which leads to debauchery. Instead be filled with the Spirit. (Ephesians 5:17-18)

The filling of the Spirit allows the Holy Spirit to accomplish the things He entered our lives to do. Through the Holy Spirit's filling, believers are empowered increasingly to walk in victory over the world, the flesh, and the devil. As a result of the filling of the Spirit our lives will exhibit what Paul called "the fruit of the Spirit"—the qualities that characterized the life of our Lord Jesus Christ when He was on earth. The Holy Spirit's filling provides us with power for service and enables us to exercise our spiritual gifts.

It is important that as we seek to find our strength in "His mighty power," we remain balanced, seeing the whole scope of the Holy Spirit's Person and work.

The Benefits of the Spirit's Filling

The filling of the Holy Spirit brings many benefits to the Christian walk.

AN INNER BENEFIT

"Do not get drunk on wine. . . . Instead be filled with the Spirit. Speak to one another with psalms, hymns and spiritual songs. Sing and make music in your heart to the Lord (Ephesians 5:18-19).

Those words hint at some wonderful, inner, and very human benefits for the believer who is experiencing the filling of the Spirit. Bible expositors have often noted the contrast between the Spirit's filling and being drunk. Not only is the contrast stated directly in Ephesians 5:18, but the initial filling of the Holy Spirit recorded in Acts 2 was misunderstood as a state of drunkenness. "Some . . . made fun of them and said, 'They have had too much wine' " (Acts 2:13). Peter responded to their misunderstanding by saying, "These men are not drunk, as you suppose. It's only nine in the morning! No, this is what was spoken by the prophet Joel: 'In the last days, God says, I will pour out my Spirit on all people' " (Acts 2:15-17).

There is a marvelous promise here for people who have tried to find their "kicks" through alcohol and drugs. Drunkenness and drug trips are illusionary experiences. They create a false euphoria that is out of touch with reality. A drunk person is controlled by a force that releases his inhibitions; his troubles seem to disappear; he gains a boldness that sometimes makes him think he can "lick" anybody in the house. The tragedy is that the euphoria is only temporary. He often awakens from his "trip" to find out that his troubles have increased. Perhaps he's been arrested for drunk driving or his wife has left him. Paul warns that the euphoria produced by alcohol produces debauchery.

Believers have an alternative that is satisfying and not illusionary. It's real. The alternative is the filling of the Holy Spirit. When He is in control, the inner benefits of love, joy, and peace prevail (Galatians 5:22). As Ephesians 5:19 indicates, the Spirit-filled believer can make music in his heart to praise God. The result is an inner calm that brings rest in even the most trying circumstances. I was once given a form of sodium pentothal as an anesthetic for surgery. I quickly lapsed into an unconscious state, but during my time in the recovery room I experienced the false euphoria that some seek through drugs or alcohol. Under the control of the drug, my mind and emotions enjoyed sublime ecstasy. I felt so comfortable, so at peace, it seemed I was floating in paradise itself. As time lapsed, however, my euphoria gave way to a sensation of pain and discomfort from the surgery. The euphoria was not real; it was only masking the real pain. Yet, the more I came to consciousness, the more quiet and at rest I felt in the Lord. Many had been praying for me, and the Holy Spirit filled me with a calmness and a joy that did not eliminate the pain but was there in the midst of it. That inner benefit needs no additional source other than the Holy Spirit Himself.

AN UPWARD BENEFIT

"Sing and make music in your heart to the Lord, always giving thanks to God the Father for everything, in the name of our Lord Jesus Christ" (Ephesians 5:19-20).

The filling of the Holy Spirit produces joyful worship. To obey these words we must be filled with the Holy Spirit. Music of praise and thankfulness to the heavenly Father flows naturally from the heart of the Spirit-filled person. When praise, worship, and thankfulness seem foreign to us, we may need a fresh filling of the Holy Spirit.

While I was pastoring in Chicago, a touch of revival visited two churches in Pekin, Illinois. Ralph and Lou Sutera, who had led in the revival awakenings that came to Regina, Saskatchewan, in the early seventies, were holding meetings there. The meetings at one church became so crowded that they had to be moved to a larger building. The meetings lasted for several weeks, dramatically affecting the lives of hundreds of believers and bringing many to Christ.

Hearing what God was doing, my wife and I decided to visit. It was a unique experience to be a part of such a powerful visitation of the Holy Spirit. As believers got right with one another and with their Lord, they were experiencing a fresh filling of the Spirit. We shall never forget the singing, the praises to the Lord, the joy, and the seemingly timeless nature of the evening. The service lasted for nearly four hours, but when it concluded people still lingered. They did not want to go home. Such revival helps illustrate the upward benefit of the Spirit's filling ministry. It allows praise, thanksgiving, and worship to flow freely.

AN OUTWARD BENEFIT

The imperative to be filled with the Holy Spirit in Ephesians immediately precedes the portions of Scripture that deal with personal relationships. Relationships between husbands and wives, children and parents, and workers and employers as set forth in Ephesians 5:21—6:9 are possible only through the Holy Spirit's filling ministry. The Holy Spirit can enable human beings to manifest a servant's heart that will make home, family, and working relationships harmonious and Christ exalting. The Spirit-filled life also prepares the believer to claim victory over Satan and his kingdom (Ephesians 6:10-18). We shall study this in more detail in succeeding chapters.

The Basics of the Spirit's Filling

"Be filled with the Spirit" (Ephesians 5:18).

What are the basic necessities for the spiritual condition the Bible calls being "filled with the Spirit"? What must I do to achieve it? How can the available, beneficial, Christ-exalting fullness of the Spirit be mine?

The Word of God keeps the formula simple. We are not talking about a condition available only to the "super saints." God means the fullness of the Spirit to be a part of the normal, daily living of every believer. What does it take to know this aspect of invincible living?

REGENERATION—FINDING NEW BIRTH (JOHN 3:1-16)

It seems wise to stress this basic point. There may be some reading these words who have never been born from above. If you were to die and stand before God and He were to say, "Why should I let you into My heaven?" would you know how to answer? Salvation—eternal life—is God's free gift to be received as your personal possession. It becomes yours the moment you reach out by faith and claim the finished work of the Lord Jesus Christ as payment for your sins.

"He came to that which was his own, but his own did not receive him. Yet to all who received him, to those who believed in his name, he gave the right to become children of God—children born not of natural descent, nor of human decision or a husband's will, but born of God" (John 1:11-13).

I recently visited a business man who received Christ as his Savior a little over one month before. Don and his family had attended our church, though he was not a believer. Much prayer and work had been exerted by the church to win him to Christ. His wife had been praying for his salvation for seven years.

When they made plans to move to another state, we invited them to our home for a farewell dinner. During the course of the evening, Don and I had a chance to talk alone. I mentioned that many of his friends hoped he might come to know Jesus Christ as his Lord and Savior before he moved away. That opened the door for conversation about eternal things, and in a matter of a few minutes, Don was praying and inviting Jesus Christ into his life to be his personal Savior and Lord.

The change was instant and profound. He immediately shared the joy of his new life with his wife, who was in another room. The next Sunday while attending church and Sunday school, he remarked that it was like someone had just turned on the lights. For the first time he could hear spiritual truth and understand what was being said. My recent visit confirmed his continued growth. Regeneration had taken place. "Therefore, if anyone is in Christ, he is a new creation; the old has gone, the new has come!" (2 Corinthians 5:17).

I was reminded again of what a truly transforming thing it is to receive Christ and to have the Holy Spirit enter one's life. All spiritual victory begins here. If any reader has not yet settled the matter of personal salvation, you must do that now. Invincible living never results from self-effort or turning over a new leaf. Victory is receiving a new life through the regenerating work of the Holy Spirit.

ELIMINATION—GRIEVING THE SPIRIT

"Do not put out the Spirit's fire" (1 Thessalonians 5:19). "And do not grieve the Holy Spirit of God, with whom you were sealed for the day of redemption" (Ephesians 4:30).

Lewis Sperry Chafer in his work *Systematic Theology* devotes one volume to the Person and work of the Holy Spirit. He devotes sixty-five pages to "Conditions Prerequisite to Filling." Nearly all of those pages are given to a study of how we grieve and quench the Holy Spirit. Dr. Chafer concludes that the filling of the Holy spirit requires only three conditions: (1) "quench not the Spirit" (1 Thessalonians 5:19, KJV*), (2) "grieve not the holy Spirit of God" (Ephesians 4:30, KJV), and (3) "walk in the Spirit" (Galatians 5:16, KJV).

Grieving the Spirit is the result of unconfessed sin in the believer's life. We are therefore confronted with a twofold problem: How can we be kept from sinning, and how do we apply God's provided cure once sin has entered our lives? The Holy Spirit is present to help us with those two major problems. If we do not utilize His Person and work to overcome the sin problem, we grieve Him. When He is grieved we will not know the victory and joy of His filling. It is of vital importance that we handle our sin problem on the basis of God's Word. That which grieves the Holy Spirit is instantly removed through confession expressed by a contrite heart. The secret is to keep short accounts with God. The moment a believer is aware of any grieving or estrangement, he needs to determine the cause and apply the remedy.

DEDICATION—YIELDING TO GOD

Quenching the Spirit refers to resisting or rejecting the will of God for one's life. Yielding to God's plan allows the Holy Spirit's filling to make us invincibly strong. Being invincible means having the capacity and power to do God's will.

Dedication involves yielding totally to God's purpose.

> Do not offer the parts of your body to sin, as instruments of wickedness, but rather offer yourselves to God, as those who have returned from death to life; and offer the parts of your body to him as instruments of righteousness. . . . I put this in human terms because you are weak in your natural selves. Just as you used to offer the parts of your body in slavery to impurity and to ever-increasing wickedness, so now offer them in slavery to righteousness and holiness. (Romans 6:13, 19)

The Holy Spirit's work is so different from that of the spirit beings over which Satan rules. Wicked spirits seek to rule our lives through

*King James Version.

subtle trickery (Ephesians 6:11) and coercive force (Ephesians 6:12). Satan desires to manipulate us and force us to accomplish his plans. The Holy Spirit does not work this way. He respects our personal dignity and gently woos us to respond to God's will. He is not interested in coercing us, but desires that we be willing responders. We do not do God's will through our own strength but through the supernatural work of the Holy Spirit within us. We must, however, yield ourselves to the Holy Spirit, expecting Him to accomplish God's will in us and through us. "Therefore, I urge you, brothers, in view of God's mercy to offer yourselves as living sacrifices, holy and pleasing to God—which is your spiritual worship" (Romans 12:1).

We must yield to the Lord and His plan in every experience of life, even the hard and the painful ones.

One of the heartbreaking stories of the Old Testament tells of the time King David fled with his family from the insurrection mounted by his own son Absalom (2 Samuel 16). As David approached Bahurim, a man from Saul's family by the name of Shimei began to throw stones at the king and his company. As he hurled his rocks, Shimei also pronounced curses upon David. "Get out, get out, you man of blood, you scoundrel! The Lord has repaid you for all the blood you shed in the household of Saul, in whose place you have reigned. The Lord has handed the kingdom over to your son Absalom. You have come to ruin because you are a man of blood!" (2 Samuel 16:7-8).

One of David's military men, Abishai, asked for permission to put an end to this indignity: "Let me go over and cut off his head" (2 Samuel 16:9).

David's response to Abishai's request might be paraphrased like this: "Don't harm him. I hear God in his words. The Lord is speaking to me in all of these happenings." What a lesson for all of us to learn about yielding to the Lord. Even in one of the most trying times in David's life, he recognized that God in His sovereignty wanted to use the experience for David's profit and His own glory.

Every battle Satan launches against us somehow fits into God's sovereign plan. Even as we resist and reject Satan's purpose in attacking us, we must yield to the lessons and purposes God has in allowing us to face the battle. Failure to seek the Lord's teaching inevitably prolongs the battle. Yieldedness says, "Lord, I hear You in this battle. I want to profit from it. I yield to what You are teaching me."

EXPECTATION—EXPRESSING OUR FAITH

"After they prayed, the place where they were meeting was shaken. And they were all filled with the Holy Spirit and spoke the word of God boldly" (Acts 4:31).

Lewis Sperry Chafer writes, "Prayer for the Spirit's filling is an error of great proportions and indicates a misunderstanding of the conditions which now obtain. The Spirit's filling does not await the influence of prayer. God is not withholding this blessing until He is prevailed upon or some reluctance on His part is broken down. He awaits the requisite human adjustments."[5]

Chafer points out that the Spirit's filling does not result from our efforts in prayer as some would seem to promote. The Spirit's filling comes as a result of God's loving gift, available to every believer as we make "the requisite human adjustments." Yet, a spirit of faith and expectancy is appropriately expressed toward the Lord in prayer. Confession and yielding to God's will too should be expressed in prayer.

The text quoted from Acts 4:31 indicates the part prayer had in the filling of the Spirit on that occasion in the life of the early church. It is entirely proper to express our expectancy for the Holy Spirit to fill us.

CONTINUATION—WALKING IN THE SPIRIT

"Those who belong to Christ Jesus have crucified their sinful nature with its passions and desires. Since we live by the Spirit, let us keep in step with the Spirit. Let us not become conceited, provoking and envying each other" (Galatians 5:24-26).

To walk in the Spirit requires moment by moment dependence upon the Spirit. We seriously err when we think we walk in the Spirit by our own human effort. We need to maintain an attitude of confidence and expectation that He will make walking in the Spirit a reality. To "walk in the Spirit" means to depend completely upon the Spirit, realizing that He alone can and will guide and help us.

What a delight it is for a parent to watch his little child learn to walk. It's always a time of much trial and error. There are many falls and failures in the process of learning to walk physically. Yet, once the skill is learned, walking becomes a practice that is done without thought.

Walking in the Spirit has a similar pattern. When we first see the need and desire to do so, the steps may seem halting and difficult. We will find ourselves resorting to serving the Lord in our own efforts. Self-effort displaces grace. Yet, when we fall, there is always forgiveness and the privilege of starting over. As we become more accustomed to the Spirit-controlled walk, we will find ourselves looking to the Holy Spirit moment by moment in every experience.

As we learn to walk in the Spirit it is excellent to begin each day

5. Lewis Sperry Chafer, *Systematic Theology*, vol. 4, *Pneumatology* (Dallas Seminary Press, 1981), 232.

with a prayer of expectancy, expressing our desire to experience the Holy Spirit's leading and enablement in every moment and happening of the day. It is also helpful to take stock in the evening as you think through the day prayerfully. Offer praise and thanksgiving for the successes realized through the Spirit's walk in you. Confess and repent of the times you relied on your own effort. This is a process that will go on as long as you live. To walk in the Spirit requires daily practice.

A Prayer for the Spirit's Filling

Loving heavenly Father, I approach You again through the Person and work of the Lord Jesus Christ. I desire to obey Your will by being invincibly strong through Your Holy Spirit's enabling power. I praise You for Your goodness in providing the Holy Spirit for my benefit and strengthening. Thank You for that day when the Holy Spirit convicted me of my need of Your salvation. I praise You that He enabled me to open my heart to the Lord Jesus Christ and Your saving grace. I welcome the Holy Spirit's indwelling presence. It is with expectancy that I receive His peace, His comfort, and His illumination of my mind enabling me to understand Your Word. I greatly rejoice in the security of His sealing work. I delight that by His baptizing work the Spirit has put me into the Body of Christ and united me inseparably with Him. I praise Your name that the Holy Spirit has brought me to spiritual life and that He will yet quicken my body at the resurrection day.

As I pray, I am increasingly conscious of my need of the Spirit's intercessions in me, through me, and for me. I pray that You will grant me the privilege of praying in the Spirit. May my thoughts and words be directed of Him. May He bring my petitions into Your presence with His perfect understanding of Your will.

I acknowledge Your plan and desire to fill me with Your Holy Spirit. Forgive me for grieving the Holy Spirit by my sinning. Enable me to appropriate more perfectly the victory You have provided for me to walk above sin and failure. Grant to me always the awareness of my sins that I might quickly confess them to You. I do not want to quench the Holy Spirit by any reluctance to submit fully to Your will and plan for my life.

Help me to see moment by moment those things You are teaching me about Yourself and Your will for my life. It is my constant desire to walk in the Spirit. I ask You to fill me with His power that You might be glorified through the invincible strength You provide me to do Your will. All of this I ask in the name of the Lord Jesus Christ for Your glory. Amen.

5

The Whole Armor of God: The Belt of Truth

> Stand firm then, with a belt of truth buckled around your waist. (Ephesians 6:14*a*)

I was standing in the cafeteria of a Christian school when a young lady approached me with some hesitancy. "Are you Pastor Mark Bubeck?" she asked. When I responded that I was, she proceeded to pull out from the stack of books she was carrying a well-worn copy of *The Adversary.* It was so tattered and worn I could scarcely believe it. "I carry this book everywhere I go," she said."I just had to thank you for writing it. It has been a tremendous help to me."

She obviously had my attention. I asked her to tell me her story. She related that before her conversion she had been deeply involved in the occult world of seances, fortune telling, and witchcraft. Because of Satan's cruel hold upon her life she began to suffer greatly, but through God's loving providence she found the only way out. She received the Lord Jesus Christ as her Savior and was born again into God's family. In time she heard God's call to Christian service and was preparing herself in Bible school for missionary work.

Ever since her conversion, but particularly after she began Bible school training, there were times when she experienced excruciating attacks from the powers of darkness that once controlled her. She related that when those attacks came, they were so fierce and sudden that they seemed to completely disarm her. They would set her reeling in such confusion and pain that she could not think what to do or say. But as each attack came on, she would gain the presence of mind to turn to one of the doctrinal prayers in *The Adversary* and verbalize the prayer in her mind, even if unable to read it aloud. As she would address the doctrinal prayer to her Lord and against the attack, she could break the attack. "These attacks are coming less and less frequently," she related. "I don't think it will be long now until that's all behind me."

A Brutal Foe

As I later reflected on that encounter, I could not but think how typical that situation was in illustrating the ruthless, cruel attack of Satan. There is significance to the first part of the believer's armor being "the belt of truth buckled around your waist." Satan is an enemy who is always ready to "hit below the belt." In the sport of boxing, or any other sport for that matter, the sense of decency and fair play outlaws hitting below the belt. If by accident an opponent happens to get the wind knocked out of him, it warrants a time out or even a penalty against the opponent who caused the injury. Most of us have had the wind knocked out of us at some time or other and remember how helpless it rendered us for a time. Only the most ruthless opponent would deliberately set out to hit below the belt.

That is the kind of foe we have. Satan makes his ways appealing to us. That is why so many get drawn into the world of spiritualism. It promises the ability to know the future, special powers other people do not have, the ability to contact a dead loved one. The appeal of Satan's promises is one of the reasons people buy occult books and magazines, pornographic literature, and pseudo-religious literature full of the "doctrine of demons." Satan makes it look appealing, but when he gets you coming his way, you begin to see how ruthless he is. "The way of the transgressors is hard" (Proverbs 13:15). "She that lives in pleasure is dead while she lives" (1 Timothy 5:6).

Believers need to know that they have a ruthless foe who hits below the belt. He will do all he can to double you over and then bludgeon your head with his destructive blows. If God has taught me anything about spiritual warfare, it is that Satan is terribly ruthless and cruel. Many of those who are deeply into the occult, if they survive, begin to search for some way out simply because their suffering is so great that they cannot endure it any longer.

I received a call from a young lady experiencing fierce emotional and physical suffering. She had a Mormon background and had later drifted into the occult. She had used the Ouija board frequently, but when she received conflicting answers at different times, she sought out a fortune teller's counsel to help her find answers to her problems.

At first the fortune teller refused to read her palm. But she finally agreed to read tarot cards for her and proceeded to describe the girl's future. Suddenly in the midst of her procedures the fortune teller quit the process, pushed the cards aside, and said, "You shouldn't be doing this. I shouldn't be doing this." She then turned, took from a shelf a copy of *The Adversary,* and gave it to the girl. "Here's a book you need to read," she said. "You're getting into trouble you don't know anything about."

Because of that response the young woman later contacted me. One can only surmise the reason that fortune teller had a copy of such a book in her possession. I dare say it was because she herself was going through torment of soul. Perhaps a Christian had given her a copy to help her see a way out.

Many of those who enter into Satan's domain find the suffering they experience absolutely ruthless in its intensity. If he makes his own followers endure such suffering, how much more ruthless would he be against those who belong to Christ, if unprotected? He will destroy you if he can.

In the words of Martin Luther's hymn, "his craft and power are great, and, armed with cruel hate, on earth is not his equal." One secret of Satan's craft is his clever use of the lie. In speaking of the devil's final end, Revelation 20:10 states: "And the devil, *who deceived them,* was thrown into the lake of burning sulfur, where the beast and false prophet had been thrown" (italics added).

The ultimate tactic of Satan's strategy is to deceive men. The Lord Jesus Christ confirmed this in John 8:44 when in rebuking the unbelieving Pharisees He said, "You belong to your father, the devil, and you want to carry out your father's desire. He was a murderer from the beginning, not holding to the truth, for there is no truth in him. When he lies, he speaks his native language, for he is a liar and the father of lies."

Whenever we are under assault from Satan, we can be sure that the lie is present someplace. Perhaps we have been deceived, and we believe something that is not true. That is often the case. Satan's roarings convince believers that they are vulnerable instead of victorious, so they succumb to fear and doubt about their position of invincible strength through their union with Christ. They believe Satan's lie, and that is the way he gains more ground against them.

There is no more important weapon than truth. We must ask the Lord daily to show us any ways we are being deceived by Satan's lies. It is also vital to ask the Lord to help us always to speak and live the truth. In warning us not to give the devil a foothold in our lives the apostle Paul also admonishes us, "Therefore each of you must put off falsehood and speak truthfully to his neighbor, for we are all members of one body" (Ephesians 4:25).

Contrary to what most of us would like to admit, the sin of lying is quite common among Christian believers. It can be such a subtle thing. Misleading statements, a deliberate attempt to leave a wrong impression, half truths, so-called "white lies," as well as outright lies are all a part of Satan's tactics to gain a foothold against us.

For years, a devoted Christian man had struggled unsuccessfully with the sin of lying. Sometimes he told inconsequential lies in ordinary conversation by adding embellishments to his stories to make them sound better. Occasionally he would tell total fabrications as true happenings to make his conversation more interesting. Afterwards he would feel guilty and ask the Lord's forgiveness, but because of the circumstances, it was often impossible for him to go back and make things right with the people to whom he had lied. It had become such an ingrained habit that he would fall into the practice before he even realized he was doing it. Finally, in desperate earnestness to be rid of this sinful habit, he began to ask the Lord to help him realize that he was about to tell a lie before he began. The Lord heard his prayer, and step by step he was able to put away the practice and to speak only the truth. It was a joy to his heart to be free of lying. In that victory he took from Satan a powerful foothold. Many of us see some degree of ourselves in the man's experience. It is God's revealed truth that defeats Satan, but giving in to deception of any kind gives our enemy an advantage against us.

Four Strongholds of Truth

The Word of God sets forth four great strongholds of truth that are part of the belt of truth.

First, the Lord Jesus Christ is the Person of Truth.

> Jesus answered, "I am the way—and *the truth* and the life. No one comes to the Father except through me." (John 14:6, italics added)

> The Word became flesh and lived for a while among us. We have seen his glory, the glory of the one and only Son, who came from the Father, full of grace and *truth.* (John 1:14, italics added)

Jesus Christ is the very embodiment of absolute truth. He is our ultimate and total protection from takeover by Satan and his kingdom. In warning the Roman believers to avoid the sinful entrapments of the world, the flesh, and the devil, the apostle Paul urged in Romans 13:14, "Rather, clothe yourselves with the Lord Jesus Christ."

As we study the armor of God, it is not surprising to see that each part of the armor is intimately related to the Person and work of

Christ. As one puts on the armor, he is in reality clothing himself with the protection of the Lord Jesus Christ.

Before his conversion, John had been deeply entrapped in drug usage. He had then got involved in Eastern mysticism. From there he had gone into witchcraft and the open worship of Satan. Through the patient, loving witness of one of his friends who had become a Christian, with painful difficulty he had come to know Christ as his personal Lord and Savior. Those who get deeply involved in Satan's realm do not easily get free enough to even comprehend the way of salvation. His conversion was an example of God's loving grace.

After his conversion, as is so often the case, Satan attacked him with devastating physical and emotional assault. In these attacks he would find himself virtually paralyzed from head to foot. Once he was unable to speak or move, Satan would torment him with thoughts like these: "You belong to us. We're going to kill you. You'll never be free. You'll never be able to work. You'd better give up. See how much power we have. This new faith will never work for you." This harassment would go on until he had lost consciousness.

Victory didn't come until he began to fight back through his mind. Even though he could not speak or move, he could still think. Aggressively he would repeat these thoughts: *I put on the Lord Jesus Christ. He is the truth. Satan, you are a liar. In the name of the Lord Jesus Christ, I command you to release my body. I give my body only to the control of the Lord Jesus Christ, and I cover myself with the shelter of His precious blood.* As he applied the truth against the enemy, he could always break the attacking power and in moments be free from the immediate attack. Applied truth protected and delivered him.

Such an extreme case reminds us that even Satan's most powerful attacks are no match for the One who is the truth. Yet, the belt of truth is something each believer must put on by his own aggressive act. D. M. Lloyd Jones in his book *The Christian Soldier* states it this way:

> The Authorized Version translation in this instance is not as good as it might be; it is misleading in the sense that it puts it in a passive way instead of an active manner. Instead of reading, "Stand therefore, having your loins girt about with truth," as if someone else did it for you, a better translation is, "Stand therefore, having girded your loins with truth." In other words, it is we who have to do this. The girdle is not put on us, we have to put it on; and we have to put it firmly in position.[1]

Objective truth must be subjectively appropriated. That is why the

1. D. M. Lloyd Jones, *The Christian Soldier* (Grand Rapids: Baker Book House, n.d.), 184.

young man mentioned above, when under fierce attack, had to aggressively act with his mind to claim and apply his victory. Victorious warfare requires our action. We cannot be passive, hoping someone else will act for us.

The Word of God is the word of truth. One argument for the inerrancy of Scripture is its own often-repeated claim to be the "word of truth." In 2 Timothy 2:15 we read, "Do your best to present yourself to God as one approved, a workman who does not need to be ashamed and who correctly handles the *word of truth*" (italics added). James reminds us, "He chose to give us birth through the *word of truth,* that we might be a kind of firstfruits of all he created" (James 1:18, italics added). The psalmist prays, "Then I shall answer the one who taunts me, for I trust in your word. Do not snatch the *word of truth* from my mouth, for I have put my hope in your laws" (Psalm 119:42-43).

It is difficult to count the number of times by direct statement or by implication that the Bible claims to be the word of truth. The Bible is the final authority for truth in our world today. The troubles of our own personal lives, the troubles of the church, and most of the troubles of the world are due to a departure from the authority of the Bible as our only infallible standard for truth. Successful spiritual warfare begins with the ultimate question. Do I accept the Bible as the word of truth, the very Word of God, as the sole and final authority of what is true and what is error? Do I accept Scripture as God's revelation? Before we can succeed in putting on the belt of truth we have to come to God's Word with the faith of a little child and look to God to receive from the Word God's divine revelation. We have to see that "the world through its wisdom did not know him [God]" (1 Corinthians 1:21), and never could. We can never trust man's wisdom and ability to reason to find truth. Truth comes by God's revelation. This is how we know where we stand; it is written in the Word. This is what we use to fight the enemy—the word of truth, the Bible. This is how we deal with temptation and judge what is sin; the Bible reveals it. This is how we face the future with confidence; we have the word of truth—God's Word—unfolding a future of total victory in Christ.

The Holy Spirit is the Spirit of truth. The Holy Spirit is the One who illumines and opens the Word of truth to our understanding and profit. This is made clear in 1 Corinthians 2:6-15, which states that natural man left to himself could never understand the Word of truth since he does not have the Spirit of truth to illumine the Word to his spiritual understanding.

> The Spirit searches all things, even the deep things of God. For who among men knows the thoughts of a man except the man's spirit within

> him? In the same way no one knows the thoughts of God except the Spirit of God. We have not received the spirit of the world but the Spirit who is from God, that we may understand what God has freely given us. . . . The man without the Spirit does not accept the things that come from the Spirit of God, for they are foolishness to him, and he cannot understand them, because they are spiritually discerned. (1 Corinthians 2:10-12, 14)

There are some important practical truths to remember as we ask the Holy Spirit to reveal God's truth to us. First, we must know that the Holy Spirit will always lead us into beliefs, actions, and attitudes that are in complete harmony with the Word of truth (the Bible) and the Person of truth (the Lord Jesus Christ). In this day of emphasis upon experience and the so-called charismatic gifts, that point needs to be carefully stressed. Those who look for extrabiblical revelations from the Holy Spirit and accept them as truth subject themselves to serious error.

I recently learned of a "spiritual leader" who stated that the Holy Spirit had revealed to her that she should divorce her husband so she would be free to give her full time to serving the Lord in her meetings. That just does not fit with passages like Ephesians 5 and Titus 2:4-5. The Holy Spirit does not lead us to violate His inspired Word.

A man attending a church I once pastored declared that the Holy Spirit had given him the gift of prophecy. He seemed most radiant with his new gift and appeared to be walking in the joy of the Lord. The problem was that his prophecies were at times in direct disagreement with God's Word. He was being deceived by his prophecies. It is little wonder that he eventually ended up with a broken marriage and a broken heart.

Second Peter 1:20-21 states, "Above all, you must understand that no prophecy of Scripture came about by the prophet's own interpretation. For prophecy never had its origin in the will of man, but men spoke from God as they were carried along by the Holy Spirit." The Holy Spirit is the author of the Word of truth, and He certainly will never tell us to believe or do something contrary to the Word of God, although the subtle deceptions of Satan might lead us to believe otherwise.

How important it is to ask the Holy Spirit to guide us into truth as we read the Word of God. The truth of our Lord and the truth of His Word will always protect us. Ask the Holy Spirit to protect you from being drawn into movements or emphases that are not consistent with His truth. As we claim the Spirit of truth to protect us daily, He will do so, because that is His ministry.

The church is the pillar and foundation of truth. The apostle Paul in instructing Timothy stated; "Although I hope to come to you soon, I am writing you these instructions so that, if I am delayed, you will know how people ought to conduct themselves in God's household, which is the church of the living God, the pillar and foundation of the truth" (1 Timothy 3:14-15).

The local church is here raised to a high level of importance in God's plan. A local church is called "God's household" and "the church of the living God." Every believer is always to be related closely to a sound, Bible-centered, Christ-exalting local church. He is to submit himself to the disciplines, the checks and balances, that God in His sovereignty builds into that local church. Many times in my own personal life, even as a pastor, the Lord has used the ministry of the church to protect me from some sad error. How many times I have seen the ministry of the local church protect a believer from total defeat. When believers rally to pray, protect, and encourage, the enemy is put to flight. Affiliate with a local church, submit to its disciplines, attend the services, and be instructed in the Word.

Satan hates to face the believer who has the belt of truth buckled around his waist. Have you ever told a lie convincingly and then suddenly the truth came out? There you were, caught in your lie, absolutely devastated. The belt of truth affects Satan and his kingdom in the same way. It devastates and totally defeats him. It exposes his deceiving, lying ways for what they are and breaks his power against you.

How does one aggressively stand firm with the belt of truth buckled around his waist? It is done by prayer. The following prayer is designed to give you guidance in claiming a vital part of the armor.

Putting on the Belt

In the name of the Lord Jesus Christ I claim the protection of the belt of truth, having buckled it securely around my waist. I pray the protection of the belt of truth over my personal life, my home and family, and the ministry God has appointed for my life. I use the belt of truth directly against Satan and his kingdom of darkness. I aggressively embrace Him who is the truth, the Lord Jesus Christ, as my strength and protection from all of Satan's deceptions. I desire that the truth of God's Word shall constantly gain a deeper place in my life. I pray that the truth of the Word of God may be my heart's delight to study and memorize.

Forgive me for my sins of not speaking the truth. Show me any way in which I am being deceived. By the Holy Spirit of truth, open the

Scriptures to my understanding and guide me into the practical understanding of His words of truth. I ask the Holy Spirit to warn me before I deceive anyone and to ever protect me from believing Satan's lies. Thank You, Lord, for making my local church a pillar and foundation for Your truth in my life. Help me to relate to my church and give protection and help to others as well as receive it myself.

I see, Lord Jesus Christ, that my ability to be invincibly strong and able to do Your will despite Satan's subtle ways requires the stabilizing power of the belt of truth. Thank You for providing this part of the armor. I take it gratefully and desire to have an ever-deepening understanding of its protection through Your power. Amen.

6

The Whole Armor of God: The Breastplate of Righteousness

> . . . with the breastplate of righteousness in place." (Ephesians 6:14*b*)

> The Lord looked and was displeased that there was no justice. He saw that there was no one, and he was appalled that there was no one to intercede; so his own arm worked salvation for him, and his own righteousness sustained him. He put on righteousness as his breastplate, and the helmet of salvation on his head. (Isaiah 59:15-17)

Warren Wiersbe's book *The Strategy of Satan* tells of a little-known character in the Old Testament, Joshua the high priest. Joshua was one of four people in the Old Testament who had a direct encounter with Satan (Zechariah 3). The story is illuminating because it shows how Satan goes for the heart of a man, the place where he is most vulnerable—where his conscience, or sense of rightness, resides.

The heart is a part of each of us that is often subject to defeat. One reason for that is our awareness of our failures, sins, and transgressions. If we do not feel guilty for sins of commission, we certainly know that we are guilty of sins of omission. Who of us can claim to meet God's standard, loving Him with all of the heart and mind and soul? Who of us ever comes close to always loving his neighbor as himself? Then there are the other sins of omission so common to God's own: neglect of prayer, careless attention to the study of God's Word, lost opportunities for witnessing to friends and fellow workers, or forgetting to pray for someone we promised to remember.

The target of Satan against Joshua the high priest was his heart, his conscience, that part of him capable of responding to God, wanting to please God. The chapter opens with Joshua standing before the angel of the Lord and Satan standing "at his right side to accuse him" (Zechariah 3:1). Satan's weapon was accusation; his plan was to indict Joshua before the Lord. Satan wants to destroy the heart of the man.

Accusing men as they approach God is another of Satan's effective weapons against believers. Our failures provide him with much ammunition.

In Revelation 12 a loud voice heralds the devil's being thrown out of heaven. "The accuser of our brothers, who accuses them before our God day and night, has been hurled down" (Revelation 12:10). Satan accuses our brothers. He accuses them before God day and night. Have you not heard him doing that to you? "How can you expect any help from God? Look at how you've failed. Look at all of those sins you've committed. Look at how you've failed to do what you know you should." On and on he goes. He wants to destroy your heart. He wants to convince you that you are such a failure that there is no use in going on. "How can God ever use such a bungling Christian as you?" More sincere Christians are defeated right here than perhaps at any other point.

The breastplate of a suit of armor is designed to protect an area of extreme vulnerability—the heart. In Zechariah 3, as Joshua the high priest is under severe attack and accusation by Satan, the Lord Himself comes to Joshua's rescue: "The Lord rebuke you, Satan! The Lord, who has chosen Jerusalem, rebuke you! Is not this man a burning stick snatched from the fire?" (Zechariah 3:2).

Joshua stands before the Lord dressed in "filthy clothes," representing Joshua's righteousness, which Isaiah 64:6 defines this way: "All our righteous acts are like filthy rags." The angel says to those near Joshua, "Take off his filthy garments" (Zechariah 3:4). Once that is done the angel assures Joshua, "See, I have taken away your sin, and I will put rich garments on you" (Zechariah 3:4). At the Lord's direction, Joshua is clothed in clean, pure garments fit to stand in the Lord's presence. He is then instructed to walk in those clean new garments in the strength and victory of the Lord. By so doing he will be a symbol of the coming servant of Jehovah, the Branch, our Messiah (see Zechariah 3:6-10).

That Old Testament story is a fitting illustration of the part of the armor now before us. The breastplate of righteousness is the only protection we have against Satan's attack on the very heart of God's servants. The Roman soldier's breastplate was of unique importance in his armor, covering his body's most vulnerable organs. Beneath the breastplate were the soldier's heart, lungs, stomach, liver, and bowels. A wound by the enemy's sword, spear, or arrow in any one of those organs meant almost certain death. For that reason, the breastplate had to be very strong and always in place.

Righteousness is thus given a place of unusual importance in the believer's warfare. There are several reasons this is so. One is that righteousness defeats Satan absolutely. Righteousness is all that Satan is not. He is unrighteous, wicked, evil, full of darkness (see John 8:44; 13:2; 1 John 3:8). Righteousness defeats Satan and turns him back.

Righteousness is also one of God's attributes. The Psalms are filled with such statements as, "your right hand is filled with righteousness" (48:10), "Righteous are you, O Lord" (119:137), "The Lord is righteous in all his ways" (145:17), and in Jeremiah "He will be called: *The Lord Our Righteousness"* (Jeremiah 23:6, italics added).

What is the breastplate of righteousness? It is the Lord's righteousness bestowed upon us and in us that protects us.

Imputed righteousness means that when I am saved, God justifies me. God the Father puts the very righteousness of the Lord Jesus to my account; it is imputed to me, put upon me by God as a judicial act. God now looks at me as being clothed in His own righteousness. In Philippians 3:8-9, the apostle Paul rejoices in this righteousness in these words, "What is more, I consider everything a loss compared to the surpassing greatness of knowing Christ Jesus my Lord, for whose sake I have lost all things. I consider them rubbish, that I may gain Christ and be found in him, not having a righteousness of my own that comes from the law, but that which is through faith in Christ—the righteousness that comes from God and is by faith." Imputed righteousness means that something that belongs to one person (Christ) is put to the account of another (the believer).

When we are justified, a marvelous exchange takes place. At the moment saving faith comes, God takes our sins *and* imputes them to Christ's account; they are seen as punished in Christ. At the same time, God also takes the righteousness of Christ and imputes His righteousness to our credit.

Putting on the breastplate of righteousness means that we are daily refreshing ourselves with the awareness of that marvelous truth. Joshua the high priest was a picture of this truth. His own filthy garments were removed and new garments, clean and worthy for the Lord's presence, were put upon him.

There is no stronger protection against Satan's accusations about our unworthiness than to keep this truth of "imputed righteousness" ever before our minds. Romans 8:1 must become a conscious, daily certainty, "Therefore there is now no condemnation for those who are in Christ Jesus." Satan will make little progress accusing us if that truth is hidden securely in our hearts and kept freshly before our minds.

God also imparts His righteousness within us. The Puritans called this *imparted righteousness.* Imparted righteousness refers to the righteousness that God puts into my conduct and life. It is no less entirely from God than imputed righteousness, but it is in the realm of my experience and is not always constant and total. Sometimes I do sanctified, righteous deeds, but at other times I do not. Genuine righteous deeds result from God's action: "For it is God who works in you to will and to act according to His good purpose" (Philippians 2:13).

In 1 Thessalonians 5:8 Paul instructs, "But since we belong to the day, let us be self-controlled, putting on faith and love as a breastplate." A superficial study might cause us to conclude that this breastplate of faith and love is different from the breastplate of righteousness. Such is not the case. Faith and love are the very best expressions of the outworking of imparted righteousness. Faith and love are righteousness at work in the believer's life.

As we put on the breastplate of righteousness we need to appreciate the importance of both our imputed righteousness and our imparted righteousness. God not only makes us righteous in our standing before Him, but He also expects that righteous deeds flow out of our lives. God's imputed righteousness is our breastplate of protection in the ultimate sense, but imparted righteousness is intended to flow from His investment.

The Breastplate's Protection

The breastplate of righteousness protects us in several ways. First, it helps give us confidence and courage. Few things are more essential to spiritual warfare than is assurance. When Satan throws his accusations against us, accusing us of our failures—which are only too obvious—it is heartening to know that it is the Lord's imputed righteousness and not our own that makes us worthy. Confidence also comes from knowing that the infused righteousness God planted in us can express itself in deeds of faith and love that glorify God. "And to put on the new self, created to be like God in true righteousness and holiness" (Ephesians 4:24).

A young man called me to express deep concern about his marriage. His young wife had shut him out of her life. She refused to seek counsel from anyone. She kept saying that the only solution to their problems was for him to leave. She suffered from a terrible inner anguish and torment and found little rest. Both of these young people were Christians, but the distance between them had widened into a great breach. Their frustrations and anger had become so intense at times that they had actually struck each other. The accuser had also been very busy in this trying relationship. The young man admitted that the call to me was a last ditch attempt on his part. Though involved in the Lord's work on a full-time basis, he was about ready to leave his wife.

As we discussed some practical steps he could take and talked about why he could be sure of victory in Christ, I could sense his confidence building. As we ended the conversation he was excited about beginning a time of fasting and prayer. Confidence and courage had received a transfusion of hope and faith. That is what the breastplate of righteousness is meant to do.

The breastplate of righteousness also allows us the opportunity to repudiate self-righteousness. As we daily claim the breastplate of righteousness we should renounce that ever-present tendency to pat ourselves on the back and say, "What a good boy am I."

Job had one of the most fearsome encounters with Satan recorded in the Word. One reason God allowed such a prolonged trial at Satan's instigation seems to have been to refine away Job's self-righteousness. As Job engaged in the early stages of dialogue with his friends, the idea that kept coming from him was, "I'm so good and right with God that I have no idea why God is allowing this terrible trial to be in my life."

A beautiful, young Christian woman in my church carried a very despondent, somewhat angry look on her face for an extended period of time. I was thankful when one day she asked to have an appointment with me. As she began to share her burdens, she talked of some deep and distressing disappointments that had come into her life. They were hard blows that had upset her emotionally. She had allowed those disapppointments to raise questions in her mind about the goodness of God. In a burst of tears she finally blurted out, "God has no right to treat me this way. I've always tried to put Him first and to keep my life free of sin. It's just not fair. It's just not fair."

As gently as I could, I tried to help her see that she was in essence saying, "God, You have no right to treat me this way, because I'm so good and so nice." When she saw this, she began to laugh and cry at the same time. Isaiah 64:6 lighted her path to repentance, "All of us have become like one who is unclean, and all our righteous acts are like filthy rags; we all shrivel up like a leaf, and like the wind our sins sweep us away." We talked about the fact that God's goodness is true whether or not our experience seems to testify to it. Goodness is the very essence of His character. When our experience does not seem to support that truth, we are to praise Him anyway.

As the Lord revealed the self-righteousness of her heart to her, a beautiful prayer of repentance ensued. She left my presence that day with a look of radiant joy.

The breastplate of righteousness is meant to do that for every believer. It provides us the daily opportunity to remind ourselves that the only righteousness we have is that which our Lord imputes and imparts to us. In times when God allows deep hurts and disappointments to come, we have the opportunity to receive them with joy. James instructs us to "consider it pure joy, my brothers, whenever you face trials of many kinds, because you know that the testing of your faith develops perseverance. Perseverance must finish its work so that you may be mature and complete, not lacking anything" (James 1:2-4). If we find ourselves drawing back from the tests the Lord allows to come, it may be that a root of self-righteousness is present. We, too, are expressing the thought, "Lord, I'm too good to deserve this kind of treatment." We must praise the Lord even for the severities of the battle.

Trusting in self-goodness is not only worthless, it also opens us up to spiritual danger. By trusting in self-goodness, an unbeliever is kept from saving faith. It is necessary to recognize one's utter sinfulness before the heart can be prepared for saving faith. In Romans, the apostle Paul draws from several Old Testament Scriptures to bring home our true condition.

> What shall we conclude then? Are we any better? Not at all! We have already made the charge that Jews and Gentiles alike are under sin. As it is written: "There is no one righteous, not even one; there is no one who understands, no one who searches for God. All have turned away and together become worthless. There is no one who does good, not even one." "Their throats are open graves; their tongues practice deceit." "The poison of vipers is on their lips." "Their mouths are full of cursing and bitterness." "Their feet are swift to shed blood; ruin and misery mark their paths, and the way of peace they do not know." "There is no fear of God before their eyes." (Romans 3:9-18)

Those words should be sufficient cause for us to repudiate self-righteousness.

Trusting in self-goodness is no less worthless after we are saved. It is still an affront to God. God will never be able to use us effectively until we see that only His righteousness is worthy.

As Jesus lived on earth, one thing Satan could never touch was His righteousness. Hebrews 4:15 declares, "For we do not have a high priest who is unable to sympathize with our weaknesses, but we have one who was tempted in every way, just as we are—yet was without sin." Neither Satan nor sin could touch our Lord's righteousness. He was tempted, but temptation was always defeated.

It is important to remember that temptation is not sin. Some Christians get upset with themselves when temptation comes. I know of a man who almost shipwrecked his life over this point. He had lived a very sensual life before his conversion, and for a time after being saved anything immoral nauseated him. It was repulsive to him, and he was thankful for the evidence of "old things passing away and all things becoming new." However, as time went on, he began to have times when the old fleshly passions were stirred anew. He would walk by a book counter displaying pornographic reading material and be tempted to pick it up. These temptations greatly distressed the man. He was sure they were a sign that he was about to return to his old ways. He reasoned that someone who has been saved and transformed should not have such temptations. He then began to think that if the thoughts were there, perhaps it would be no less evil to do the acts he once had done.

At that critical moment a Christian friend pointed out to him that temptation to do evil is not sin. Christ Himself was "tempted in every way, just as we are—yet was without sin" (Hebrews 4:15). That knowledge proved to be of great comfort to that Christian brother. Temptation in and of itself does not soil righteousness. It is only when we entertain the temptation and lust after the object that sin invades our lives.

When we become believers, a threefold process of sanctification is set in motion. First, in our position with God we are immediately sanctified ("set apart") and declared to be righteous. That is called imputed or positional sanctification. The righteousness and holiness of Christ is credited to our account, and the Lord looks upon the believer as a "saint," even though in conduct he may not be very "saintly."

Sanctification is also a process that goes on throughout the believer's lifetime. As the apostle Paul closes his first letter to the Thessalonians he expresses the plea, "May God himself, the God of peace, sanctify you through and through. May your whole spirit, soul and body be kept blameless at the coming of our Lord Jesus Christ. The one who calls you is faithful and he will do it" (1 Thessalonians 5:23-24). That process is sometimes called "growing in grace" and is carried on by assimilating God's Word through the agency of the Holy Spirit (Romans 15:16; 1 Corinthians 6:11; Philippians 2:12; 1 Timothy 4:7; 1 Peter 2:2).

The process of sanctification never ends or reaches perfection in this life. That is why we must claim the breastplate of righteousness on a daily basis. We all need to keep growing toward that measure of the stature of the fullness of Christ in our conduct as well as our standing (Ephesians 4:11-12; Colossians 3:5,8,12-14).

Our final sanctification will come when our Lord returns. First John 3:2 states, "But we know that when he appears, we shall be like him, for we shall see him as he is." At that moment, our sanctification in body, soul, and spirit will reach its total fulfillment. What God began at our conversion will be made complete.

The importance of putting on the breastplate of righteousness in an aggressive, active way cannot be over-stressed in spiritual warfare. The victory of our Lord's righteousness and the defeat it brings Satan and his kingdom must be aggressively applied and not passively assumed. This victory belongs to us, but we must lay hold of it.

The Danger of Passivity

I was seeking to motivate a Christian lady to active aggressive warfare. She had been in a fierce battle with Satan's kingdom for a number of years. A background of occult practice and very sinful living had characterized her life before her conversion. The harassment and suffering she endured from Satan had left her weary, worn, and feeling anything but aggressive. Passiveness is always a dangerous state to be in when it comes to spiritual matters. "It's the Lord's battle," she said to me. "If I'm going to have victory in this fight, the Lord will have to do it." We need to depend on the Lord for the ultimate victory, but we have to participate in the battle. We must not be totally passive.

Let us imagine that a soldier finds himself in the best-equipped army in the world. The latest weapons, the strongest armored tanks, and the most powerful rockets and bombs are at his disposal. But suppose that soldier goes out to face his enemy leaving his guns and other equipment behind. What will happen? Somebody with less equipment can easily strike him down. Having the protection is not enough; he must use it.

The application is obvious. We are members of God's army. We are to endure as good soldiers of Christ. We are equipped with all the armaments we need to defeat the enemy of our souls and his entire kingdom, but we must use them. The breastplate of righteousness is one of the most vital. We must claim its protection daily and aggressively use it to resist the devil and put him to flight.

Claiming the Breastplate

In the name of the Lord Jesus Christ, I put on the breastplate of righteousness. In this moment, I repudiate any dependence I may have upon my own goodness. I embrace the righteousness that is mine by faith in the Lord Jesus Christ. I look to the Holy Spirit to be effecting righteous actions, pure thoughts, and holy attitudes in my life. I hold up the righteous life of the Lord Jesus Christ to defeat Satan and his kingdom. I affirm that my victory is won and lived out by my Savior. I eagerly ask and expect that the Lord Jesus Christ shall live His righteousness through me. Through the precious blood of Christ, cleanse me of all my sins of omission and commission. Let me walk in a holy and clean manner that honors God and defeats the world, the flesh, and the devil, through Jesus Christ, my Lord. Amen.

7

The Whole Armor of God: The Shoes of Peace

> And with your feet fitted with the gospel of peace as a firm footing. (Ephesians 6:15)

> Peace I leave with you; my peace I give you. I do not give to you as the world gives. Do not let your hearts be troubled and do not be afraid. (John 14:27)

Have you ever experienced the loss of your sense of peace? What a time of panic, fear, and torment that brings. A dark time in my life still lurks in my consciousness as one of life's most fearsome moments. It happened in the early years of my marriage. I was in my second year of seminary, taking a full academic load, working part time, and struggling financially to make ends meet. There were some unresolved conflicts in my spiritual life, and they were putting greater emotional and psychological pressure on me than I realized. Suddenly one day, as a result of a minor crisis, something snapped in my emotional well-being, and total panic swept in. Words fail to describe the darkness, the terror, that comes to the human soul and spirit when fear begins to reign. Only those who have gone through such a valley will understand the hellish nature of the experience.

A similar experience happened to Charles Haddon Spurgeon following a speaking engagement at the Surrey Gardens Music Hall. As Spurgeon was speaking to an overflow crowd of more than 10,000 people, someone screamed "fire" and started a stampede for the exits. In the ensuing chaos, seven people were trampled to death and a great many suffered serious injury. Mr. Spurgeon went into dark depression. He describes the crisis in these words:

> I refused to be comforted; tears were my meat by day, and dreams my terror by night. I felt as I had never felt before. "My thoughts were all a case of knives," cutting my heart in pieces until a kind of stupor of grief ministered a mournful medicine to me. I could have truly said, "I am not mad, but surely I have had enough to madden me, if I should indulge in meditation on it." I sought and found a solitude which seemed congenial to me. I could tell my griefs to the flowers, and the dews could weep with me. Here my mind lay, like a wreck upon the sand, incapable of its usual motion. I was in a strange land, and a stranger in it. My Bible, once my daily food, was but a hand to hit the sluices of my woe. Prayer yielded no balm to me; in fact, my soul was like an infant's soul, and I could not rise to the dignity of supplication. "Broken in pieces all asunder," my thoughts, which had been to me a cup of delights, were like pieces of broken glass, the piercing and cutting miseries of my pilgrimage.[1]

God's servants are not immune from such dark trials. Adding to my own trauma was the feeling of dread and humiliation that I was going to have a "nervous breakdown." To me, that would be the worst thing that could possibly happen to a young man preparing for the ministry. *This can't be happening to me. I've never had a nervous day in my life. How can I ever be fit to comfort and counsel others in their spiritual and emotional needs when I've fallen apart in my own life?* Thoughts like those were constantly with me. The only way to describe my torment during those days is to say that I was experiencing a total loss of my peace. My prayers, though desperate, seemed locked away from God's ears. The Scriptures, though often read, were like dead words to my troubled mind and emotions.

During those days, how thankful I was for a patient, prayerful, understanding wife and for Dr. Vernon Grounds, the godly president of the seminary I attended, who was a refuge of great comfort. As a trained psychologist, he was able to help me sort through some of the spiritual conflicts of my life. The trauma went on for several weeks, however, and seemed not to lessen in intensity. The extended time only added to my ultimate fear of having a total nervous collapse. How I longed for peace and wondered if it would ever return to my tormented life.

During that time, I learned that one of my professors had gone through a similar trial when he had been in seminary. Just knowing that someone else had experienced such a trial and survived comforted me. With a flicker of hope, I sought him out. He was most understanding and encouraging.

I expressed my fear of experiencing a "nervous breakdown," per-

1. Charles H. Spurgeon, *Charles Haddon Spurgeon: Autobiography,* vol. 2, *The Full Harvest, 1861-1892* (Carlisle, Pa.: Banner of Truth, 1975), 195-96.

haps ending my hope of ever being a minister. With kindness he spoke words that shocked me into a sudden awareness of truth. He said, "Mark, if God wants you to go through a nervous breakdown, you ought to want to have a nervous breakdown more than anything else in the world."

Those words stopped me. I did not hear anything else that was said. Truth had slain my pride and fear.

Excusing myself hurriedly, I made my way home to get alone with God. On the way, I remembered having prayed during a special prayer day at seminary, "Lord, while I'm in seminary, do in my life whatever You see needs doing to prepare me to be a usable servant." Those words now rushed back to my consciousness with new insight into what my trauma was all about.

I knelt in prayer that afternoon and, for the first time since the trauma began, felt I could commune with God. With quiet surrender I prayed, "Lord, You know I've feared and fought even the thought of having a nervous breakdown. I've not even considered that it might be in Your will to train and discipline me. Forgive me for my self-will and obstinate pride. Lord, You know I really don't want to go through a nervous collapse, but if You want me to, then here we go. I'm ready." At that moment I was sure that God was going to take me through such a breakdown, but instead, as I arose from my knees, I noticed the return of at least a portion of inner peace. As I continued to surrender to the Lord's perfect will, that peace kept growing. In a few weeks I was fully recovered.

What great lessons that experience taught me. During that traumatic time, God built into me a tenderness and an understanding for people going through emotional crisis that I could never have learned any other way. He taught me the absolute necessity of full surrender to His will, even if it threatens my own desires. But perhaps the greatest lesson of all was to learn the value of peace.

Through the apostle Paul, the Holy Spirit describes peace as the shoes of the soldier in warfare. No part of a soldier's dress is more important than his shoes. Have you noticed that if your feet hurt, you hurt all over? A severe corn on the little toe or a troublesome bunion can hurt so much that you just can't walk anymore, let alone fight. In spiritual battle likewise, if you are hurting, you are not going to be an effective soldier.

Good shoes are necessary for good footing. A Roman soldier with sword in hand needed to have under him shoes that gave him traction, stability, and sure footing, He could not fight a battle if his feet were easily knocked from under him. Again the application to spiritual warfare is obvious. If our shoes of peace are not secure and well-fitted, we will not long endure the battle the enemy presses against us.

A soldier's shoes give him ease of movement so that he will be ready to meet any challenge. In life we need different kinds of shoes for different kinds of activity. The track runner needs light, well-spiked track shoes to move rapidly over the cinders. The basketball player needs shoes with specially-designed soles to keep his feet from sliding on the polished boards. The heavy construction worker would probably soon injure his feet if he wore dress shoes while guiding his jackhammer.

Similarly, we need a certain kind of shoes for spiritual battle. The only shoes that will see us to victory are the shoes of peace, and these have some important characteristics that must be understood and faithfully claimed by the invincible servant of the Lord.

Positional Peace

Romans 5:1 declares, "Therefore, since we have been justified through faith, *we have peace with God* through our Lord Jesus Christ" (italics added). This kind of peace is not subjective, experiential peace; it is objective, legal fact. The only way you gain this peace is to know it in your mind and receive it by faith. Through God's decree of justification, you have peace with God. That means God is not angry with you anymore. The war between God and the believer has ended.

Many years ago I heard a pastor preach on the subject of justification. He likened the word *therefore* to God's finger pointing back to the cross and the perfect work of redemption accomplished there. Therefore, because of the cross, because of what God did there to satisfy His own anger against sin, because of the full price Christ paid to take away all of our sin, because God reconciled the believing sinner to Himself, we are justified. Justification includes not only the removal of all of our sin but also the addition of all the righteousness of Christ Himself. God robes us in His righteousness. Therefore, because God, in His own work and plan, has justified us, we have *peace with God.*

Peace with God is meant to bring peace to the believer's intellect, his mind. Justification is not an experiential, feeling-based truth. The only way believers know we are justified—declared righteous in God's sight—is because God says so and we believe Him. Inner peace comes when we accept the plain fact of what God has done. As a result, we have peace with God.

An incident comes to mind out of the life of a young friend. He was going through several trials. Discouraged because of the prolonged nature of the testings, he said to me one day, "I guess God is punishing me for something. I don't know why He's angry at me, but if He wants to be angry that's OK because He does everything well."

My young friend's attitude was commendable, but his theology was terrible. God does not pour His anger upon His own children. He does not punish us in the sense of punitive hurt. The Lord chastens or disciplines His own to correct them, but He does not judge or punish His servants. That was settled at the cross of Christ. Now all believers are justified. As a result we all have peace with God.

Knowing and living in the reality of this truth is so important to invincible warfare. The mind needs to lay hold of this great fact. We must walk in the shoes of peace with God. If the soldier is always ill at ease with the thought that God may be angry with him or that he has to toe the mark to keep God's anger way, he will make a poor soldier.

Experiential Peace

Philippians 4:6-7 reads, "Do not be anxious about anything, but in everything, by prayer and petition, with thanksgiving, present your requests to God. And *the peace of God,* which transcends all understanding, will guard your hearts and your minds in Christ Jesus" (italics added).

If peace *with* God is an intellectual peace, the peace *of* God is an emotional, experiential peace. We can know all the facts about God's provisions, but if emotions do not support our knowledge, we will not be able to act upon what we know to be true. The peace of God applies a balm of inner serenity to our emotions. If you have the peace of God, you feel at peace in mind and heart—the total inner person.

All of us know what it is like to lack inner peace. Some crisis comes into our lives—some worry, some danger—and a turbulent storm rages within. Many people seek peace through tranquilizers, depressants, and other drugs. Others turn to illicit drugs or alcohol. Some try pseudo-religious movements such as transcendental meditation to find a solution for their lack of peace.

The God-Prescribed Tranquilizer

How does the believer walk in the shoes of peace? Philippians 4:6-7 reminds us that it is through prayer. Time alone with God in thankful, prayerful petition is the most effective inner tranquilizer. There is no solution to inner disquiet as effective as prayer. It always works. "Do not be anxious about anything," the imperative commands us. The peace of God transcends all understanding. That means the peace of God is above and beyond what we understand. It is more than we really need to see us through. It is an overflow.

The next time you sense a great inner shaking or even just a slight inner disquiet, try prayer. Shut yourself away for thirty minutes or an hour alone with God. Use doctrinal praying. Pray back to God the truth of being "in Christ," inseparably united to Christ in all of His Person and work. Pray through your understanding from the Word of the Person and work of the Holy Spirit. Pray on each part of the believer's armor. Thank the Lord for all of His grace and goodness. Tell Him about your anxieties and concerns. God will intervene to change things. It may be so gradual you will scarcely know how or when it happens, but when you finish you will discover the peace of God within your emotions. A quiet inner serenity and calm reigns even though the storm may still rage about you. I know that to be true both by experience and by the truth of the Word of God. In fact, if you are practicing this kind of praying regularly, you will discover the peace of God already there when the crisis happens.

A few years ago I sensed the Lord calling me to a special time of fasting and prayer. Not knowing the Lord's purpose, I determined to fast for three days. When fasting, I usually try to set aside the times I usually would be eating to pray. At the close of the second day, at the dinner hour, I had just finished a time of prayer when my wife called me to the phone. It was a long distance call from my oldest brother, informing me that both of my elderly parents had been killed in a single car accident. For a moment there was the stunned disbelief such news would bring to anyone, but suddenly I was aware of an inner peace that passed all understanding. The peace of God was already there like a reservoir of supply to keep my heart and mind through that trial. That peace was so great that I was able to bring a devotional message at my parents' funeral.

The Scriptures are utterly practical and workable. The Bible works when we use its promises in every circumstance of life.

Have you ever considered that your lack of inner peace may be God's way of calling you to prayer? We have many marvelous electronic gadgets available to us today. One of the most fascinating is that little "beeper" radio that many doctors, businessmen, and even pastors carry to enable people to signal them wherever they are. Several doctors in the church I pastor keep their beepers with them when they come to church. Sometimes while we are at worship, a beeper will sound and the doctor signaled will quietly get up and leave.

A lack of inner peace could be God's beeper signal to you. God may be calling you for an audience with Himself. He wants fellowship with you, and in the process He will restore to you that peace that transcends all understanding.

Peace That Protects

Philippians 4:9 states; "Whatever you have learned or received or heard from me, or seen in me—put it into practice. And the *God of peace* will be with you" (italics added).

I recalled hearing a gifted Bible teacher tell an experience that has left a great truth lingering with me. It seems his young son was having difficulty with a bully who would pick on him as he went to school. The boy talked it over with his father, and they decided the best course of action would be just to ignore the bully. That seemed only to make the bully more bold. Every day as the boy walked to school the bully would tease and shove him, laughing at him for being too much of a coward to fight.

The boy and his father talked it over again and decided that maybe the best thing to do would be to accept the bully's challenge to fight. Even though the bully was bigger, perhaps when he saw that the little fellow had some fight in him, he would show his own cowardly streak. But the problem got only worse because the bully beat up the boy quite badly, and soon he was afraid to go to school at all.

Finally in desperation, the father decided he would just take his son by the hand and walk with him to school. An amazing thing happened. His little son, who was totally afraid to walk alone to school, put his hand in his father's hand and walked with his head held high. The bully was in his usual place ready to pounce on his victim, but when he saw that six-foot dad the bully ran away. Without saying a word, the son looked at his father and smiled a big smile of relief. The bully never again gave him any trouble.

The application is obvious. The bully we face, our enemy Satan, and his kingdom are too great for us to face alone, but when *the God of peace* is with us, we need have no fear. As Paul closes the book of Romans, he states, "The *God of peace* will soon crush Satan under your feet" (Romans 16:20, italics added).

The Security of Obedience

How do we maintain a walk in the shoes of peace? Proverbs 16:7 states, "When a man's ways are pleasing to the Lord, he makes even his enemies live at peace with him." That proverb harmonizes with Philippians 4:9. Both texts stress obedience. As a believer seeks to walk in obedience to his Lord, the special protective presence of the God of peace abides with that believer. Disobedience will make us vulnerable to the attacks of Satan.

Lack of obedience in the life of King Saul was the reason God removed His protection from Saul and let him fall victim to his enemies. One instance is recounted in 1 Samuel 15, where Saul is said to have kept certain of the animals of the Amalekites, which God had ordered utterly destroyed. When Saul excused his lack of obedience by insisting that he only kept the animals to sacrifice them to God, Samuel's reply was devastating. "Does the Lord delight in burnt offerings and sacrifices as much as in obeying the voice of the Lord? To obey is better than sacrifice, and to heed is better than the fat of rams. For rebellion is like the sin of divination, and arrogance like the evil of idolatry. Because you have rejected the word of the Lord, he has rejected you as king" (1 Samuel 15:22-23).

What important words for us. "These things happened to them as examples and were written down as warnings for us, on whom the fulfillment of the ages has come. So if you think you are standing firm, be careful that you don't fall!" (1 Corinthians 10:11-12). The presence of the God of peace with us to make us invincibly strong has to do with a walk of humble, dedicated obedience. Rebellion, disobedience to God's will, makes us vulnerable to defeat.

If you are resisting God's will, you must deal with that resistance. Defeat for you and victory for your enemy will soon result unless the God of peace is put in control.

Jesus Christ—Our Peace

"But now in Christ Jesus you who once were far away have been brought near through the blood of Christ. For he himself is our peace" (Ephesians 2:13-14*a*). Our shoes of peace rest upon the relationship we have to the Person of peace. The Christian faith is not primarily a system of doctrines and dogmas believers follow, though it certainly includes rich doctrine. The Christian faith is primarily a relationship with the Person of the Lord Jesus Christ. "He himself is our peace."

Each part of the armor in its ultimate application remains the Person of Christ. When we walk in peace, we are walking in Him. Only in Him are we justified and have peace with God. It is in Christ that we are able to pray and receive answers that bring us the peace of God. Christ is the only one ever perfectly obedient to the God of peace. Ultimately our obedience is possible only because we are "in Him." It is perfect obedience that is credited to our account. As we by faith allow Him to live His life in us, experiential obedience in our lives glorifies Him.

There is nothing more foundational to successful warfare than having the right shoes on our feet—the shoes of peace. Peace with

God, the peace of God, the God of peace, and the Person of peace, the Lord Jesus Christ, are the essentials of shoes that enable us to firmly stand.

Satan's attempts to defeat us are seldom more obvious than when he attacks our sense of peace. His strategy is to create chaos within a person. A universal characteristic of those under Satanic or demonic attack is the turmoil, the disquiet, the torment, the lack of peace they endure. The demonic man of Gadara described in Mark 5 is a tragic study in the extent of the lack of peace Satan can generate.

Satan is also a false peacemaker. Satan and his kingdom offer pseudo-solutions for peace in abundance. Illicit drugs, alcohol, and tranquilizers dull the human consciousness into a stupor of blissful peace, but when they wear off, the torment is so severe that one is driven again to seek relief through his false peace. Exotic religious systems abound today, promising their adherents a special peace if they will only follow these cults. For a time false peace seems to work, but ultimate chaos is always near at hand.

Those who followed Jim Jones and his People's Temple cult all told of the meetings where Jim Jones presided that were so wonderfully warm and happy. One participant observed that while attending the meetings he "felt so good inside." But the feeling turned out to be Satan's false peace. History has never recorded a more discordant, terror-filled, notorious end to a cult than the murder-suicide deaths of nine-hundred and ten people in the jungle of Guyana. One of the army men who saw that awful scene in Jonestown observed, "There were no Bibles." That really tells the story. When men twist the Word of God or throw away the Word, they throw away the only source of true peace.

Appropriating Peace

Loving heavenly Father, by faith and in the name of the Lord Jesus Christ, I put on the shoes of peace. I accept Your declaration that I am justified and that I have peace with You. May my mind grasp that wondrous truth with ever increasing awareness. I thank You, Lord, that I need not carry any anxiety or suffer from inner torment or turmoil. Thank You, Lord Jesus Christ, that You have invited me to make all of my needs known to You through prayer. Teach me to wait in Your presence until the inner peace of God, which transcends human understanding, replaces my anxiety. I desire to know the strong presence of Your peace. May You walk with me and say to me, "Don't be afraid; I will help you."

With all of my heart I want to be obedient to Your will at all times.

May the fullness of Christ who is my peace enable me to so walk in Him that the fullness of His peace may glorify God through me. I take the shoes of peace in the name of the Lord Jesus Christ, and by faith I shall walk in them this day. Amen.

8

The Whole Armor of God: The Shield of Faith

In addition to all this, take up the shield of faith, with which you can extinguish all the flaming arrows of the evil one. (Ephesians 6:16)

On our twenty-fifth wedding anniversary, my wife and I were seated next to the plate glass window of the restaurant atop the John Hancock Building in Chicago, then heralded as the world's tallest building. The shoreline of Lake Michigan stretched before our gaze and combined with the majestic skyline of Chicago to make our romantic evening delightful. As we relived our twenty-five happy years together, we failed to notice an approaching thunderstorm. Suddenly we were jarred by a blast of lightning followed almost instantaneously by a thunderous roar. Our table—in fact, the entire restaurant—seemed to tremble. From the vantage point of our window table, we watched the storm rage with startling fury. The clouds were inky black. The rain swirled and churned in the wind and seemed to burst against the glass in a fierce effort to reach us. The flashing lightning and roaring thunder continued to add brilliant color and stereophonic sound to the drama of shrieking wind and splashing rain. It was a bit unnerving for a time; then the thundershower passed as suddenly as it had come, and the setting sun returned to paint its glory on the departing clouds.

I have since reflected upon how that experience illustrates the shield of faith. We could see the storm, even feel something of its fury, but it could not reach us. We were shielded by heavy plate glass engineered to meet just such storms.

The shield of faith is an important part of the believer's armor. "In addition to all this," the text says, we are to take the "shield of faith." The importance of the shield is seen in the words "with which you can extinguish *all* the flaming arrows of the evil one" (italics added). That is about as inclusive as it can be. *All* of the blazing missiles of the kingdom of Satan can be extinguished, quenched, put out by the protection of the shield. From behind the shield, you can sometimes see Satan's arrows streaking toward you. You can sometimes hear the thunder of his roar and feel the trembling of his fury, but the shield is strong enough to endure Satan's rage.

Shielded in Every Direction

One reason the shield of faith is so critical to the believer's walk is that it provides *complete* protection. The Greek word for shield, *thureos,* conveys the idea of a large shield. You might picture it as a shield that thoroughly encapsulates you. Psalm 5:12 states; "For surely, O Lord, you bless the righteous; you *surround* them with your favor as with a shield" (italics added). The psalmist saw God's shield literally surrounding the righteous, protecting them from all directions. The Lord's protection is in front of us, behind us, above us, beneath us, on our right hand, and on our left. God's shield provides thorough protection.

A few years ago we toured the Space Center Museum at Huntsville, Alabama. We were fortunate to have a dear friend, Alfred Finzel, escort us on the tour. Al, now retired, was one of the German scientists who worked so successfully with Werner Von Braun in our country's space program. One of the fascinating exhibits of that museum features the space capsules of the various moon probes. The environment of space is so hostile to human life, the scorching heat of re-entry into the earth's atmosphere so intense, that no human life could survive without the "every direction shielding" of those space capsules. That pictures the believer's shield of faith. The hostile atmosphere of Satan's kingdom is too deadly for us to survive without the shield.

Before he was allowed to tempt Job, Satan complained to God, "Have you not put a hedge around him and his household and everything he has?" (Job 1:10). God's shield was there to protect Job from the hostile atmosphere of Satan's hate and rage. The story of Job proves that Satan would torment and kill all of the righteous if it were not for God's shielding. We shall have more to say later about how Satan's efforts were able to pass through that shield in some measure and why, but at this point it is good to note how high and adequate was God's hedge.

The Object of Our Faith

A further reason the shield is so critical to victory is seen in the object of our faith. Our faith is not our shield, but rather the object of our faith is our shield. Faith in and of itself can provide no protection if the object of the faith is faulty.

Some of us recall the civil war that raged in Zaire while it was still the Congo. Under Moishe Tshombe, foreign mercenaries were hired to put down the rebellion. The professional, well-trained soldiers were more than a match for the poorly trained rebel Congolese soldiers. As they were pushed back farther and farther by the mercenaries, the rebels began to flee in fear. In desperation, the rebel leaders promoted a scheme. A witch doctor's concoction that looked like white ashes was to be spread all over the bodies of the rebel soldiers. They were assured that this concoction would shield them from the bullets of the mercenaries. Bravely, with complete faith in this new "magic shield," many of the rebels made a stand, sometimes exposing themselves openly to the mercenary marksmen. They were sure they would be shielded by the "magic ash," but of course they were soon cut down by their enemies' bullets. Their faith failed because the object of their faith had no power to shield them. Proverbs 30:5 states, "Every word of God is flawless; he is a shield to those who take refuge in him."

Faith is merely the means the believer has of appropriating the shield. God is the object of our faith. He is the shield.

Confidence in the Shield

A third reason the shield is critical to our victory is that it provides the believer with the *confidence* of protection. Does the presence of the shield mean that Satan will never be allowed to touch us? Some people seem to think so. The story of Job should forever lay to rest such thoughts. Satan was allowed to get through to him. The believer has no assurance that he will not experience some of the same kinds of trials from Satan's kingdom.

How can we explain such happenings if the shield of faith is able to quench *all* of Satan's fiery darts?

The answer can be found only by carefully examining the sovereign workings of our Lord. Satan's blazing missiles are always intended to hurt and destroy the believer. He is absolutely ruthless and devastatingly cruel in his attacks.

A fine Christ-centered family wrote to me of their troubled college-age daughter. She showed evidence of being a dedicated believer in the Savior. Attractive and brilliant, on intelligence tests she scored near the genius level. Her future seemed bright until she was faced with Satan's challenge. Let me quote from her mother's letter:

> She began having very troubled nights and would often come running in terror to our bedroom, saying she had a nightmare and wanted to sleep on the floor of our bedroom. . . . She told us really hair-raising tales of nightly visits from Satan, who would taunt her and attempt to goad her into accepting both his physical 'love' and his way of life. . . . She is now living with a sister, who has told us that she does not sleep at night anymore, but stays awake all night and then sleeps in the daytime. Until two weeks ago, she could not be alone in the evening or night, as her terror was unbearable. She told her sister that she was seeing not only Satan but many demons at night in her room. She said that these demons rushed around the corners of her room and crawled up her bedposts to peer into her face.

How hideous and tormenting Satan can be. In this girl's case, her Christian psychiatrist recognized that she "was having identity problems and also was experiencing demonic oppression." Satan's ultimate purpose is to destroy, to tear down, to afflict, to torment, and to kill us if God would permit. Concerning Job, God said to Satan: "He is in your hands; but you must spare his life" (Job 2:6). This leaves little doubt that apart from God's shield Satan would have killed Job as he did Job's family.

The Lord's Purpose in Battle

But what of God's purpose, we must ask? That God sometimes does let Satan afflict believers despite the shield of faith and the rest of the armor is obvious both in the Word of God and in life. What is God's purpose and what happens to Satan's missiles?

As Satan's fiery darts penetrate the shield of faith—if in God's sovereignty He allows them to do so—they cease to be Satan's flaming missiles. Rather, they become the refining and purifying messengers of God's love.

Fire can destroy, or it can refine. Some friends had a fire hit their apartment building. The next morning I walked with my friend through the remains of his burned-out apartment to see if we could salvage anything. The destruction was terrible. Everything was burned. All of their lifetime keepsakes, all of their clothing.

Yet fire can be purifying too. I recall as a youth melting down lead to be poured into various shapes and molds. I loved to get the torch so hot that the molten metal seemed transparent. The hotter it got, the more latent impurities would rise to the top and have to be skimmed off, always leaving the metal purer than it was before.

That illustrates what God is doing as He lets some of Satan's fiery darts pass through His shield. Under His sovereign eye God never lets Satan's work go any further than He intends. James 1:2-4 says, "Consider it pure joy, my brothers, whenever you face trials of many kinds, because you know that the testing of your faith develops perseverance. Perseverance must finish its work so that you may be mature and complete, not lacking anything." First Peter 1:6-7 states, "In this you greatly rejoice, though now for a little while you may have suffered grief in all kinds of trials. These have come so that your faith—of greater worth than gold, which perishes even though refined with fire—may be proved genuine and may result in praise, glory and honor when Jesus Christ is revealed."

Consider the assurance of 1 Corinthians 10:13, "No temptation has seized you except what is common to man. And God is faithful; he will not let you be tempted beyond what you can bear. But when you are tempted, he will also provide a way out so that you can stand up under it."

Staying God-Centered

We must remain God-centered and never become Satan-centered. That is always a danger. We must not become so conscious of Satan's power that we are always "fighting the devil" instead of "serving the Lord."

Again, Job is a good example for us. All of Job's sufferings and problems were directly from Satan's hands. Yet, as Job discusses his torment with his three friends and even with the Lord, his thoughts, words, and hopes were God-centered. Job never even credited Satan with producing his affliction. He kept his eyes upon the Lord, and ultimate victory came.

When under Satan's attack—even while we are resisting him and his purposes—we need to be thanking God for His purposes in allowing the battle. Satan means to produce evil and hurt, but God purposes to refine the believer and make him a stronger servant. Through Jeremiah, the Lord said to Israel, "Like clay in the hand of the potter, so are you in my hand" (Jeremiah 18:6). That is a biblical principle we must respect and never forget. Just as controlled fire is one of man's greatest assets, so the controlled fires of Satan's afflictions in God's hands are in our lives for good.

A pastor recently told me about his work with a woman who had experienced years of terrible satanic affliction. It extended back into her childhood. She remembered that uncontrollable rages would sweep over her at the most unexpected moments. In adulthood, the problems worsened. A difficult marriage, unfaithfulness that led to adultery, and the resulting guilt added to the problem. After her husband's death, desperate to find answers, she got involved rather deeply in spiritism. That involvement accelerated her difficulties with the world of demons.

Just entering the bathroom would trigger vulgar thoughts, and obscene language would pour from her mouth. Voices from the spirit world would ceaselessly torment her, demanding and cajoling her to certain actions. When the experiences had reached a zenith, the pastor came on the scene. The woman's first response was to avoid him—at the prompting of the voices—but during a painful attack she finally turned to the pastor for help.

Not sure how to proceed, he spent considerable time seeking to lead her to Christ but encountered fierce opposition by the powers of darkness. As the way of salvation was explained to her, she found the harassing voices and confusion almost unbearable. They could only proceed with much patience and prayer. Finally, a breakthrough came, and she was able to pray to receive Christ. Great relief and calm ensued but did not last long.

The pastor related that a copy of *The Adversary* had come into his hands, and with some believing friends he sought to free this suffering woman from her torments. They boldly encountered the enemy. Several demonic powers identified their presence and were commanded to leave. Several sessions of prolonged prayer and warfare were necessary, but today that woman is free, rejoicing in the Lord. Sometimes she can still hear voices, but they are far away and barely audible, as if a great shield is between her and their presence. Before they left, some threatened to return if she ever backslid and gave them a chance, but she is determined to memorize the Word and walk with her Lord. She has resolved to keep her mind centered upon the Lord and His Word, and not upon the enemy. That is one of the keys to continual victory. We must never become preoccupied with the enemy but instead be totally occupied with the Lord and His Word.

The Deadly Nature of the Battle

We must recognize the deadly nature of the battle the believer is in. Various translators use graphic language to describe what Satan shoots at us. "Flaming arrows," "fiery darts," "blazing missiles" all convey the sneaky, deadly serious nature of the evil one's intent.

The tactic of using flaming arrows in warfare is almost as old as war itself. In the days of walled cities, if attacking troops could shoot enough flaming arrows over the walls to start fires, their battle was easier. If the troops inside the city were occupied with putting out fires, they would not be able to guard against the advancing troops.

That is very similar to Satan's strategy against us. He likes nothing better than to keep us busy fighting fires rather than resisting him and keeping our attention upon our Savior. His purpose is not only to destroy, but to divert us—to create panic and terror. If he can get the city afire and divert our attention, he will then be able to walk in and take over.

The threat of fire is real to many who live in the beautiful canyons of southern California. That was particularly true in the late summer and fall of 1978. Heavy rains in the early spring had created a lush growth of grass and brush on all the hillsides. The dry summer months and the Santa Ana winds off the desert had made every canyon a potential fire trap. Terrible fires swept through several canyons, burning hundreds of beautiful homes in a few moments of time. The fierce heat caused almost everything in the path of the fire to fairly explode. Yet, there were some homes that were spared, usually because the owners had devised a method of shielding their homes from the flames. One such homeowner had devised an extensive sprinkler system, driven by a gasoline powered pump that drew water from the family swimming pool. As the fires approached and the air was full of blazing missiles driven by the high winds, the sprinkler system was activated, thoroughly drenching the house, the roof, the bushes and trees, and the area around the home. The missiles were all quenched as they fell on the shield of water. Though every other house in that area was consumed, the one with the carefully prepared shield of water was untouched. Reading that account in the newspaper, I could not help but see the comparison to spiritual warfare. The presence of the shield does not stop the blazing missiles from being thrown, but it does insure that no damage will result. All of them are quenched.

Appropriating the Shield

Let us now consider what this shield is and how we appropriate its protection. The shield of faith in its fullest meaning is the sovereign omnipresence of our triune God.

God made a promise to Abraham: "The word of the Lord came to Abram in a vision: 'Do not be afraid, Abram. I am your *shield,* your very great reward' " (Genesis 15:1, italics added).

Through Moses, God said to Israel, "Blessed are you, O Israel! Who is like you, a people saved by the Lord? He is your *shield* and helper and your glorious sword. Your enemies will cower before you, and you will trample down their high places" (Deuteronomy 33:29, italics added).

In one of David's songs of praise he sang, "The Lord is my rock, my fortress and my deliverer; my God is my rock, in whom I take refuge, *my shield* and the horn of my salvation. . . . You give me your *shield* of victory; you stoop down to make me great" (2 Samuel 22:3,36, italics added). There are more than a dozen references in the Psalms to the fact that the Lord Himself is our shield.

Satan is a created being, unable to overcome the Person and presence of the Lord. It is of great comfort to know that our shield of faith is the formidable power and Person of the Lord Himself.

Through faith, we are aware of the presence of the Lord between us and the enemy. Notice that the shield is "the shield *of faith*" and that the text says, "With which *you* can extinguish all the flaming arrows of the evil one" (Ephesians 6:16, italics added). *You,* the believer, have something to do with the extinguishing of the flaming arrows, and the shield *of faith* requires our active faith for its effectiveness.

We must actively participate in our warfare. The shield's protection is something we must take and use on a daily basis.

Some believers question the necessity of putting on each part of the armor daily. "Why should I so often go through an act of aggressively taking or claiming my armor? Won't it become a habit or 'vain repetition'?"

I often encounter such questions and remind those asking that none of us would think of not dressing daily simply because doing so is repetitious. We put on clothing because we do not want to be embarrassed by our nakedness as we go out to face the world. How much more we need spiritual dress. Much more is at stake than just embarrassment. We are in a war with a deadly enemy who will take advantage of missing armor.

You may say, "Well, why did the Lord plan it that way? Why didn't He provide me with armor that I don't have to claim on a daily basis?" The answer to that may be seen, in part, in God's provision of manna in the Old Testament. The Lord wanted the Israelites to gather it daily. Any excess gathered, except for use on the Sabbath, always spoiled. It had to be freshly gathered to sustain life and provide blessing. Each daily gathering reminded the people that it was from God; it was His provision, evidence of His goodness. Our Lord builds into all of His dealings with us provisions that require daily communion and daily appropriation of His grace. There may be times when we will put on each part with haste and slight thought. Yet, there will be other times when we carefully meditate upon the significance of each part of the armor, resulting in loving worship of our Lord.

Guarding Angels

Angels exercise a much more important part in shielding us than most of us realize. Hebrews 1:14 states, "Are not all angels ministering spirits sent to serve those who will inherit salvation?"

The psalmist promised, "For he will command his angels concerning you to *guard* you in all your ways" (Psalm 91:11, italics added).

In such texts the term *guardian angel* takes on relevant meaning. The angels exercise a vital role in fulfilling God's sovereign plan to shield us from Satan's darts. As spirit beings, the holy angels are not limited to the physical world as we are. They see the fallen angels as they attack us and are able to advance against them.

A striking picture of the ministry of shielding angels is seen in the story of Elisha in 2 Kings. The king of Aram wanted to work his strategy against the king of Israel, but every time he made plans the king of Israel knew about them and frustrated him. Furious, the king of Aram was sure that some of his own men were cooperating with the king of Israel. One of his officers replied, "None of us, my lord the king . . . but Elisha, the prophet who is in Israel, tells the king of Israel the very words you speak in your bedroom" (2 Kings 6:12).

Upon learning this, the king of Aram sent a strong contingent of armed and mounted troops to surround the city of Dothan and to capture and destroy Elisha.

The next morning when Elisha's servant saw the city surrounded he was exceedingly fearful, but when he told Elisha, the prophet was calm. "Don't be afraid," the prophet answered. "Those who are with us are more than those who are with them" (2 Kings 6:16).

Elisha asked the Lord to let his servant see the protection of the angelic host, and suddenly the servant saw the hills full of horse-drawn chariots of fire all about Elisha. As the enemy troops approached, they were stricken with blindness by the Lord's host and diverted away in defeat.

Angels are more active in our affairs then most of us ever realize. Hebrews 13:2 reminds us, "Do not forget to entertain strangers, for by so doing some people have entertained angels without knowing it." Angels enter into battle with the powers of darkness in Daniel 10. The holy angel who came to Daniel had met in combat a fallen angel called "the prince of the Persian kingdom." Even Michael, one of the chief holy angels, got involved, and reference is made to a further battle with the Prince of Persia and the Prince of Greece (Daniel 10:15-21).

In taking your shield of faith, ask for the presence of the holy angels to protect you. Knowing the angels are in the hills about you as you face your enemy is very reassuring. Elisha was not in any more need of protection than we are. Anyone doing the Lord's business is a target for destruction.

The Blood of Christ

We must never forget that the blood of Jesus Christ is the basis for the believer's acceptance by our holy and righteous heavenly Father. "In him we have redemption through his blood, the forgiveness of sins, in accordance with the riches of God's grace. . . . But now in Christ Jesus you who once were far away have been brought near through the blood of Christ" (Ephesians 1:7; 2:13). Verses like these harmonize with 1 Peter 1:2, 19 and Hebrews 9:7-14 to establish that it is through the blood of Christ that God is able to accept us.

The blood of Christ has a powerful effect in defeating Satan. In Revelation 12:11 a loud voice from heaven proclaims Satan's defeat and the victory of the redeemed in these words, "They overcame him by the blood of the Lamb and by the word of their testimony; they did not love their lives so much as to shrink from death."

Christ's death through the shedding of His blood effectively shields us. Hebrews 2:14-15 states, "Since the children have flesh and blood, he too shared in their humanity so that by his death he might destroy him who holds the power of death—that is, the devil—and free those who all their lives were held in slavery by their fear of death."

What a perfect and complete shield we have. It extinguishes all the flaming arrows of Satan, if we use it. Failure to use the shield will allow some of Satan's fiery darts to work against believers.

Taking Up the Shield

Loving heavenly Father, I take by faith the protection of the shield of faith. I count upon Your holy presence to surround me like a capsule, offering total protection from all of Satan's flaming arrows. Grant me the grace to accept Your refining purpose in allowing any of Satan's arrows to pass through the shield, and even to praise You for it. Help me to concentrate upon Your presence and not the enemy's arrows.

In the name of the Lord Jesus Christ I claim the protection of the holy angels to guard and shield me from the assaults of Satan's kingdom. May these ministering angels be present to interfere with the strategy of Satan to harm me and my family. I appropriate the victory of the blood of the Lord Jesus Christ and hold it against the advances of the evil one. With gratitude and praise, in the name of the Lord Jesus Christ I rejoice in Your victory. Amen.

9

The Whole Armor of God: The Helmet of Salvation

Take the helmet of salvation. (Ephesians 6:17*a*)

Do not conform any longer to the pattern of this world, but be transformed by the renewing of your mind. Then you will be able to test and approve what God's will is—His good, pleasing and perfect will. (Romans 12:2)

In *The Strategy of Satan,* Warren Wiersbe relates the four times in the Old Testament when Satan made a direct approach to people. The first study deals with the temptation of Eve in the Garden. The first strategy of Satan, as recorded in Genesis 3:1-7, was centered upon Eve's mind. The apostle Paul sees this approach as one of Satan's chief strategies. 2 Corinthians 11:3 states, "But I am afraid that just as Eve was deceived by the serpent's cunning, your *minds* may somehow be led astray from your sincere and pure devotion to Christ" (italics added).

The Mind Under Siege

Satan's target is our minds. His weapons are his subtle and clever lies (Genesis 3:1-7; John 8:44; Romans 1:25). His lies are so clever that we have little defense against them unless we soundly know the truth. Satan wants to keep us ignorant of God's truth so that he can control our minds.

A Canadian father with a broken heart came to see me. A man in his late sixties, he told me the sad story of his daughter.

In her youth and teen years, his daughter had been a brilliant student. She had captured most of the academic prizes throughout her years of formal education. Her skill at typing allowed her to come within a hair's breadth of setting a new world record for typing speed. She was full of happiness and had a zest for living that made her attractive to everyone.

But inside her heart was a void; an emptiness that she longed to fill. By his own admission, her father was at least an agnostic, if not an outright atheist. His marriage had ended in divorce, and close family ties were severely strained. With no spiritual values, his brilliant daughter began to search for something to fill the spiritual void.

She studied Eastern mysticism and became deeply involved in the Hare Krishna movement. She pursued transcendental meditation with evangelistic fervor for a time and married a man involved in the study of Eastern mysticism. Her five thousand dollar savings account was given to him so that he might go to India and study under a renowned teacher. Upon his return from that study, they both began to experiment with the occult, becoming involved in seances and other practices of witchcraft. When some frightening experiences with the spirit world began to plague her during this experimentation, she had a superficial Christian experience that she called being "born again." It seems certain that it was not the spiritual "rebirth" our Savior spoke about. The fruit of that experience was extreme fanaticism and continued sinful living.

Confusion began to rule her mind. She could not hold a job and was in and out of several mental hospitals. She and her husband lived together only sporadically. Her baby had to be taken from her because of her neglect, and she readily offered the child up for adoption. Though her brilliance was still obvious, her mind seemed not her own. Outside voices told her what to do, and her confusion left her a helpless soul, unstable and unable to function. The distraught father, still an unbeliever, asked if the church could be of any help to his daughter.

Cases like this one are multiplying in our time. I am presently working with at least a half dozen cases that are almost identical. Good minds, often brilliant minds, become hopelessly confused and disoriented. Too many times the one troubled is unwilling to seek help on his own. He cannot understand why anyone is upset by his erratic behavior. He just wants to be left alone so that he can get on with his irresponsible living. When this happens, such a person becomes a terrible burden to his family and to society.

The apostle Paul seems to have had such situations in mind when he told Timothy to "gently instruct" such people "in hope that God will give them a change of heart leading them to a knowledge of the truth, and that they will come to their senses and escape from the trap of the devil, who has taken them captive to do his will" (2 Timothy

2:25-26). The emphasis upon "gently instruct," "knowledge of the truth," and "come to their senses" seems to indicate that the problem is one of deception; they have believed something that is false to be true.

To bring back someone from such a state, first be sure that he is genuinely saved. Next, put him under the care of a well-grounded Christian. Systematic teaching of the truth of God from the Bible, memorization of large portions of the Word, and careful instruction in spiritual warfare are the three most important steps in helping a person to get free from such problems.

Protecting the Mind

Physically, man's head is one of his most vulnerable parts. Soldiers are not the only ones who have to wear helmets. Construction workers, motorcycle riders, football players, and even baseball players when at bat wear protective helmets. If the head is severely injured, the rest of the body soon begins to malfunction.

Recently a young man in our church was injured in an industrial accident. A heavy barrel fell forty feet, breaking his back in several places. Despite the severe injuries to his body, he probably would have recovered if not for the terrible injury to his brain. When the brain began to fail, it was not long until the rest of the body organs began to fail and death ensued.

In spiritual matters, the same holds true. If Satan can capture the mind with his lies, he begins to control and destroy the whole person. If the mind goes, everything goes.

During seminary days I worked in construction on a government project. One rule was firmly imposed. No one could be anyplace on that large construction project without his helmet. Not wearing it was cause for immediate dismissal. With that same kind of urgency, the apostle Paul instructs us to wear our helmet of salvation.

Many biblical passages warn us that our minds are vulnerable to the subtle ways of Satan. James 1:8 warns that a "double-minded man" is "unstable in all he does." To be double-minded is to try to live with two minds. It is a kind of spiritual schizophrenia; the mind divides itself into two parts. One part believes truth, and the other part believes Satan's lies.

When David prayed, "Give me an undivided heart, that I may fear your name," he was showing his awareness of the problem of double-mindedness in spiritual matters (Psalm 86:11). We must also be aware of the tendency to have faith here and not have faith there, to be willing to be victorious here but be sinful there, to want to do God's will to a certain point but not to want God's will beyond that. If Satan cannot control all of your mind, he is quite content to take the part you will let him have. He knows he will get more later.

Satan's Strategies to Control the Mind

Ephesians 2:1-3 makes clear that prior to our conversion we were under the control of "the ruler of the kingdom of the air, the spirit who is now at work in those who are disobedient" (Ephesians 2:2). Colossians 1:21 tells us that "Once you were alienated from God and were enemies in your *minds* because of your evil behavior" (italics added).

Romans 8:6-7 states, "The mind of sinful man is death, but the mind controlled by the Spirit is life and peace, because the sinful mind is hostile to God. It does not submit to God's law, nor can it do so." Just as Satan is the enemy of God, so his control makes our minds God's enemy.

Satan can control the mind of a Christian. Ananias and Sapphira were true believers and a part of the early church. They met with God's severest discipline, death, because, as Peter says, "Satan has so filled your heart that you have lied to the Holy Spirit" (Acts 5:3). Satan attacks the mind of believers relentlessly and ruthlessly. He seems to have the power to project his thoughts into our minds so that we think his thoughts are our thoughts. That was true of Ananias and Sapphira. They thought the scheme to keep part of the money for their property, while telling the disciples they were giving it all to the Lord, was their own idea, but it was not. It was Satan's lie, projected into their minds, and they believed it and acted upon it.

A Christian brother shared that he was troubled by thoughts that often came while he was praying. He would suddenly begin to think, "Pray to Satan! Pray to Satan!" He felt terrible guilt that such hideous thoughts could be in his mind. He was greatly relieved to see that the thoughts were projected into his mind by Satan's kingdom and he was not responsible for them. He was responsible only to resist and reject them and to command the powers of darkness to leave him, in Jesus' name, and to go where the Lord Jesus Christ would send them.

Jesus Christ as Our Helmet

When the aged Simeon took the baby Jesus into his arms and praised God, one of his expressions of praise was, "My eyes have seen your salvation" (Luke 2:30). Salvation was a Person that Simeon could see and hold in his arms. The psalmist declared, "The Lord is my light and my salvation" (Psalm 27:1). Peter proclaimed, "Salvation is found in no one else" (Acts 4:12). Salvation is a Person more than a condition or a state of being.

A friend of mine has spent most of his life witnessing for Christ to the Jewish people. If a Jewish person says to him, "The name Jesus isn't even once stated in the Old Testament as the name of Messiah," he delights in turning in the Hebrew Bible to a verse of Scripture that has the word *salvation* in it. If they know enough Hebrew he asks them to pronounce the word *salvation* in Hebrew. The word is *Yeshuah,* meaning safety, deliverance, or salvation, and *Yeshuah* is also the way to pronounce the name *Jesus* in Hebrew. Every time a Hebrew reads the word *salvation* in the Hebrew language, he is saying the name *Jesus.* Joseph was told by the angel concerning the child to be born of Mary, "You are to give him the name Jesus, because he will save his people from their sins" (Matthew 1:21). He is our salvation; salvation is a Person.

True salvation requires someone else to rescue you from a situation in which you are helpless. When I was young, on a very hot summer day I went swimming with a number of my brothers and cousins in the local gravel pit. The water, though very cold near the bottom, was well-warmed by the sun on the surface and ideal for swimming. We decided to swim across the pit, a distance of fifty yards or so, to see who could make it the fastest. I was not then a very good swimmer, and when I started to fall behind and get tired, I decided to turn back and swim to the starting point. But I was tiring very rapidly, and panic began to set in, adding to my fatigue. I wondered if I would make it. Finally, when my strength seemed drained, I thought I was near enough to the shore to quit swimming and walk on in. My feet went down but there was no bottom. I went under. My feet finally hit bottom, and I pushed myself to the surface. With water in my lungs, too weak to swim, I was going under a second time when a man on the shore saw me. Quickly he stepped into the water, thrust out his strong hand toward me, and I grabbed it with all the strength I had left. He pulled me to shore, and I was saved. He was my salvation. There was no way I could have done one thing further to save myself. At that moment I needed a savior to prevent me from drowning.

That is true of everyone who is saved from his sins. We were lost and undone. We were going down for the last time and could not do one thing to rescue ourselves. We needed salvation—a Person to reach out His nail-scarred hands and save us from perishing forever. That's what Jesus Christ did. He is our salvation.

After becoming believers, there are still areas in which we are helpless to save ourselves. One of those areas is the mind. We need the helmet of salvation to protect our minds from the projected thoughts and attitudes of Satan and his demon powers.

How the Helmet Protects

The best way to keep Satan's thoughts out is to keep Christ's thoughts in. As surely as Satan can "fill [our] hearts," so much more can the Lord Jesus fill our minds with His thoughts. Unlike Satan, however, the Lord Jesus does not intrude where He is not invited. That's why it is up to us to invite the Lord Jesus Christ to enable us to think His thoughts after Him. It is one of those responsibilities of grace that is our moment by moment duty. It is why we memorize God's Word. It is part of putting on the armor.

Throughout the day, then, one should be alert to maintain that stance of faith. The moment a thought comes to mind that we recognize to be of the flesh or of Satanic origin, it is good to say: "In the name of the Lord Jesus Christ I reject this thought as being wrong. I ask my Lord Jesus Christ to replace it with His thoughts."

There is no surer way of putting the mind of Christ within us than by putting His Word into our minds. We often say that Jesus Christ is the living Word of God and the Bible is the written Word of God. Scripture offers a marvelous correlation between the Person of Christ and the Word of Christ.

When one memorizes the Word of God, he is actually putting within his mind the mind of Christ. That Word becomes a helmet of salvation to the mind and heart. David found that out long before Jesus came to earth. "I have hidden your word in my heart that I might not sin against you" (Psalm 119:11). David was putting the mind of Christ within him even before the Person of Christ had been revealed through the incarnation. If you are serious about protecting your mind from Satan's control, you must fill it with God's Word.

Lester Roloff of Corpus Christi, Texas, had a remarkable ministry with delinquent boys and girls, dope addicts, and alcoholics. Many chaotic lives came to order and healing through his homes. One key to his success was firm discipline administered in love. Residents had to comply with discipline: to avoid all substances that have a narcotic affect upon the body, to respect authority, to work and study, to worship and pray, and most important to memorize the Word of God. They committed to memory entire chapters of the Word of God. The lives that have been dramatically turned around through this ministry are a testimony to the importance of getting the Word into the mind.

The power of God's Word is essential to spiritual warfare. Those tormented by Satan's attack upon their minds need God's Word in their minds. The most effective thing you can do for someone so tormented is to help him memorize Scripture.

Hope Shields the Mind

In 1 Thessalonians 5:8-9 the apostle Paul states, "But since we belong to the day, let us be self-controlled, putting on faith and love as a breastplate, and the *hope* of salvation as a helmet. For God did not appoint us to suffer wrath but to receive salvation through our Lord Jesus Christ" (italics added). Here the helmet of salvation is described as the hope of salvation.

Have you ever been lost in a forest? It is a very frightening experience. While on an elk hunting expedition, I once got lost for the better part of a day. As we left camp that morning, our guide pointed toward a basin several miles above timberline and explained that we would meet there sometime in the afternoon. If any of us got separated from his hunting partner, he was to head for that basin. He promised to meet us there and guide us back to camp.

We were instructed to keep a couple hundred yards between us so that we might better stumble onto an elk. But that made it difficult to keep one's hunting partner in view, and it was not long until my partner and I were separated. The forest was so vast I could no longer see that distant basin. On top of that, clouds covered the sun, and my sense of direction was gone. My only encouragement that I was going in the right direction was that I kept going uphill. After several hours of walking and climbing, I was not interested so much in hunting as in just hoping that someone would find me. I did not have a clue as to how I would ever find my way back to camp.

Finally, I broke out above timberline, saw the basin, made my way there, and sat down on a large rock to wait. Several hours passed, but no hunters appeared. To add to my anxiety, the sky darkened and it began to snow lightly.

I am sure that at that moment I would have panicked if it had not been for one fact. I had hope that my guide would come for me. He had promised. He had told us where to wait. I was sure that I was at the only rocky basin in that whole area and, therefore, he must come even though it seemed past time for him to be there. The snow kept falling harder. I was feeling the cold and knew that if a heavy snow fell, I would be hopelessly lost and would probably die of exposure without help. It was hope that my guide would come that kept me confident.

Finally, late in the afternoon, far below, I could see a man climbing toward me. It was our guide. He had kept his word. The rest of the hunters had turned back because of the snow, but he had come on with my hunting partner to find me. I was so glad to see them. I had developed high altitude sickness from overexertion and would never have walked out alone. By morning, over two feet of snow had fallen on our camp, and we had to depart from the mountains before we were snowed in.

That experience helps to illustrate the hope of salvation. Christ is our salvation and our hope. He is coming to rescue us. At the moment of His return that will be true, but it is also true in every experience of the believer's life. Just when we feel the most lost and forsaken, just when the enemy seems to be winning the day, just when the storm is heaviest, the hope of salvation comes to lead us back to safety. If the helmet of salvation is covering our minds, we need never lose hope. We always know He is going to come. He knows where we are. "God has said, 'Never will I leave you; never will I forsake you.' So we with confidence say 'The Lord is my helper; I will not be afraid. What can man do to me?' " (Hebrews 13:5-6).

The writer to the Hebrews asks a searching question of believers. "How shall we escape if we ignore such a great salvation? This salvation, which was first announced by the Lord, was confirmed to us by those who heard him" (Hebrews 2:3). That question is pertinent to spiritual warfare. God has provided the helmet of salvation; we must take it. We must not passively assume our salvation but aggressively *take* Him, His mind, His Word, His power, and His presence. The emphasis is not on being saved from our sins but rather on what is available to us since we have been saved. It is a salvation of protection, insuring victory over the attacks and pressures of Satan's kingdom.

Putting on the Helmet

Loving heavenly Father, I take by faith the helmet of salvation. I recognize that my salvation is the Person of Your Son, the Lord Jesus Christ. I cover my mind with Him. I desire that He put His mind within me. Let my thoughts be His thoughts. I open my mind fully and only to the control of the Lord Jesus Christ. Replace my own selfish and sinful thoughts with His. I reject every projected thought of Satan and his demons and request instead the mind of the Lord Jesus Christ. Grant to me the wisdom to discern thoughts that are from the world, my old sin nature, and Satan's kingdom.

I praise You, heavenly Father, that I may know the mind of Christ as I hide Your Word within my heart and mind. Open my heart to love Your Word. Grant to me the facility and capacity to memorize large portions of it. May Your Word be ever over my mind like a helmet of strength, which Satan's projected thoughts cannot penetrate. Forgive me for my neglect, my failure to aggressively take the salvation always available to me. Help me to fulfill the discipline of daily duty to appropriate Your salvation. These things I lay before You in the precious name of my Savior, the Lord Jesus Christ. Amen.

10

The Whole Armor of God: The Sword of the Spirit

> Take . . . the sword of the Spirit, which is the word of God. (Ephesians 6:17*b*)

When the apostle Peter made his great confession to the Lord Jesus, "You are the Christ, the Son of the living God," the Lord Jesus made a very challenging response: "And I tell you that you are Peter, and on this rock I will build my church, and the gates of Hades will not overcome it. I will give you the keys of the kingdom of heaven; whatever you bind on earth will be bound in heaven, and whatever you loose on earth will be loosed in heaven" (Matthew 16:16,18-19).

That is a promise setting forth the opportunity every believer has to aggressively overcome Satan's kingdom. Ours needs to be much more than merely a defensive battle. We have opportunity to be aggressive and actually to invade Satan's kingdom. Hell, or Hades in this text, refers to the unseen world of fallen beings. For a number of years I saw that passage only as a promise from our Lord to protect His church from the attacks of Satan. That thought is certainly there, but the promise goes far beyond that. The Greek word *katischuo,* translated "overcome" or "prevail," literally means "shall not prove stronger." The primary purpose of Satan's gates is to protect what he claims as his own. He wants to hold onto what belongs to him and build such strong gates that we cannot get any of what he claims away from him. Our Lord is saying that His church will be able to go right through those gates and take from Satan what he would like to keep as his own.

Binding and Robbing Our Enemy

When the Pharisees accused Jesus of driving out demons by the power of "Beelzebub, the prince of demons," both Matthew and Mark record that our Lord knew their thoughts and showed that Satan's kingdom could not stand if it were as divided as they said (Matthew 12:22-29; Mark 3:22-27). He then made a most dramatic statement that applies to our victory over Satan. "How can anyone enter a strong man's house and carry off his possessions unless he first ties up the strong man? Then he can rob his house" (Matthew 12:29). As believers, united with Christ in His authority, we are able to so war against Satan that we can bind him, tie him up, and rob or take away what he wants to claim as his own.

Our stance is not to be one of merely protecting ourselves, as important as that is. We are to see ourselves as invincible soldiers of Christ who can advance against this "strong man," Satan, invade his domain, and take away from him those people and spiritual fortifications he claims. The other parts of the armor in Ephesians 6 are mainly protective and defensive, but now we come to see that our spiritual sight must extend beyond the defensive stance. The "sword of the Spirit" is an aggressive weapon as well as a means of defense.

The analogy of a human army may serve to help us see this truth. Suppose a modern day army were to specialize only in defense. The troops would have the strongest, most bullet-resistant helmets available. Each soldier would be equipped with vests that could not be penetrated by modern rifles. They would have tanks with the thickest armor, jet fighters with the fastest speed and maneuverability, and every other protective weaponry imaginable. There is only one problem. This defensive army has no bullets, no guns, no rockets, no bombs, or artillery. What would happen to such an army against an aggressive enemy? That enemy, though not as well-equipped defensively, will just keep pounding away at the defense, and eventually the pounding will get through. The old adage "The best defense is a good offense" has application in spiritual warfare too. "For though we live in the world, we do not wage war as the world does. The weapons we fight with are not the weapons of the world. On the contrary, they have divine power to demolish strongholds" (2 Corinthians 10:3-4). Though Satan presses a relentless battle against every believer, the believer who sees that he is responsible to carry the battle to the enemy is the one who wins.

A Christian man experiencing a severe battle with Satan and his demon kingdom sought my counsel. The powers of darkness were suggesting to him such thoughts as "Curse God," "Tear up the

Bible," "Set the church on fire," and others of an even more vulgar nature. After carefully teaching and encouraging him in his warfare, I instructed him to get very aggressive against the thoughts that seemed demonic in origin. I urged him when such thoughts came to say something like this: "I reject these thoughts to curse God and choose instead to honor the Lord. In the name of the Lord Jesus Christ, I bind the power of darkness that projects these thoughts into my mind, and I command you and all who work with you to leave me and to go where the Lord Jesus Christ sends you."

His response was typical of many people who are under such oppression. He had been intimidated so long by the fierce opposition of Satan that he said to me, "Can I do that? I'm afraid to do that. I'm just a man, and Satan is so powerful."

Satan would like to keep us thinking in such error. He always wants to keep us from going on the offensive.

Our Offensive Weapons

We have essentially two offensive weapons to use against Satan. They are the Word of God and prayer. In the days of the early church, the apostles were leading the fight, carrying the battle to the enemy, and invading his gates. You cannot do that without a proper emphasis upon the offensive weapons. Acts 6 describes what happened when the need arose for someone to take over the daily distribution of food to widows. The church chose the first representatives for church ministry so that the apostles might "turn this responsibility over to them and . . . give [their] attention to prayer and the ministry of the word" (Acts 6:3-4). Progress in the Lord's work requires an aggressive use of prayer and our sword, God's Word.

The sword is last on the list of the parts of armor. Why would that be?

For one thing, we are not ready to use our aggressive weapon against Satan's kingdom until all of the other parts of the armor are in place. None of us is ready to march into battle without our armor. The sword is listed last as a warning against presumptuous, foolhardy warfare. In our bold view of invincible warfare we must never forget who our enemy is. He is the most powerful of all created beings. He was a formidable foe to even Michael, the archangel. "But even the archangel Michael, when he was disputing with the devil about the body of Moses, did not dare to bring a slanderous accusation against him, but said, 'The Lord rebuke you!' " (Jude 9). That verse comes in a section warning those who "reject authority and slander celestial beings" (Jude 8).

Though we have authority as believers to be bold and fearless in our battle with Satan, we do not have the right to be flippant or presumptuous. The basis of our victory is that we are united with Christ, who has defeated Satan. Even the Lord Jesus in His encounters with Satan resisted the devil with dignity and proper respect for Satan's created role (Matthew 4:1-11). As mentioned in chapter 3, Acts 19:13-20 provides an illustration of some people who went into battle with the powers of darkness in a presumptuous and foolhardy way. The seven sons of Sceva, a Jewish chief priest, saw Paul invoking the name of the Lord Jesus Christ over people who were demonized, thus setting them free from their bondage. They believed that they too might use the name of the Lord Jesus to deliver people so afflicted and tried to use the formula "In the name of Jesus whom Paul preaches, I command you to come out." The response from the demon was clear: "Jesus I know and Paul I know, but who are you?" At that point, the man controlled by the wicked spirit "jumped on them and overpowered them all. He gave them such a beating that they ran out of the house naked and bleeding" (Acts 19:13-16).

The message of this incident ought to be clear. One cannot trifle with Satan's kingdom. Although the men were probably not yet believers in the Lord Jesus Christ, the warning has application to true believers today. A careless, unprepared advance against Satan's kingdom that lacks full awareness of our union with Christ, the ministry of the Holy Spirit, and the provision of our armor may prove disastrous.

Missionaries have got into trouble by careless approach to the battle. I have known of several who have experienced severe problems when they treated such things lightly. One missionary friend had dismissed fetishes and wooden idols dedicated to Satan worship as having little significance. Upon the conversion of a witch doctor, he asked to have the witch doctor's fetishes and idols to keep and show as missionary artifacts. The consequences almost proved permanently disastrous. Afflictions and severe problems came upon him and his family. The oppression was devastating. It appeared for a time that he would not be able to continue his missionary service. Finally the items were burned, and he sought the Lord's forgiveness for his careless attitude about the realness of Satan's power.

The Power of God's Word

The sword of the Spirit is the *Word of God.* In keeping with John 1:1, the Lord Jesus is often spoken of as "the living Word" just as the Bible is the written Word. We have to be careful, however, not to deify the written Word to the point that we worship it. We must worship not the Bible, but the God of the Bible. Yet, because it is the very Word of God and will never pass away, the Bible carries many of the attributes of God Himself.

It is the eternal Word just as God Himself is eternal. As God is omnipotent, so does His Word have all power to defeat Satan and to accomplish God's will. As God is immutable, so the Word of God will never change. As our Lord is omnipresent, so His Word is always there and ready to be used in every situation. As God is holy, so His Word is holy. The writer to the Hebrews says: "The Word of God is living and active. Sharper than any double-edged sword, it penetrates even to dividing soul and spirit, joints and marrow; it judges the thoughts and attitudes of the heart" (Hebrews 4:12).

The Inner Working of the Word

The sword of the Word has the power to penetrate one's life. It is meant to do corrective surgery within the soul, spirit, thoughts, and attitudes of the believer. That is perhaps the secret of its power against Satan. As the believer uses it, the Word can penetrate, cleanse, and change the believer's life and in so doing, cut away Satan's grip upon that life.

Nothing is quite as important in spiritual warfare as getting the Word of God into the mind and heart of the believer. That one thing will accomplish more in setting a person free from Satan's oppression and affliction than any other method I know.

A Christian brother who had come under severe oppression from the enemy was for years unable to work or to attend church. He withdrew from life and duty. Fear, depression, and torment seemed to rule his life. Then victory began to come as he started memorizing large portions of God's Word. Daily he meditated on Scripture portions and repeated their meaning. It was amazing to see the change that simple procedure effected in his life. Anyone who is serious about spiritual warfare must memorize the Word and meditate upon it daily, even hourly.

There is no substitute for persistent, steady, consistent application of God's Word against Satan. The Lord Jesus Christ used that approach in His dramatic encounter with Satan in the wilderness, recorded in Luke 4:1-3.

He had fasted for forty days. At the end of that time Jesus was hungry, and food was many miles away. Satan tempted our Lord, saying: "If you are the Son of God, tell these stones to become bread" (Matthew 4:3). In reply, Jesus quoted from Deuteronomy 8:3, "It is written: 'Man does not live on bread alone' " (Luke 4:4).

Next Satan tried to tempt the Lord Jesus to take a shortcut to the glory of His coming kingdom by worshiping him. Once again Christ quoted the Word: "It is written: 'Worship the Lord your God and serve him only' " (Luke 4:8).

The final temptation came at the highest point of the Temple in Jerusalem, where Satan tried to get Jesus to "throw yourself down from here." That time, Satan himself quoted the Scriptures, from Psalm 91:11-12. Once again the Lord Jesus Christ persistently used the weapon of the Word, quoting Deuteronomy 6:16, "It says: 'Do not put the Lord your God to the test' " (Luke 4:12). At that point, the devil left Jesus "until an opportune time" (Luke 4:13). He was defeated by the Savior's persistent use of the "sword" but was determined to try again.

The servant of Christ will find Satan using the same pattern of attack against him. And Satan will leave only as the Word of God is persistently applied against him.

Guidelines for Using the Sword

One of the most obvious requirements for using the "sword" is to *know the Word of God.* It was the accepted practice for devout Jewish boys of our Lord's era to memorize the first five books of the Old Testament. For most of us, that would seem an impossible task, yet there are people living today who have committed the entire New Testament to memory. Others know large portions of both Testaments. It seems obvious that the Lord Jesus Christ's ability to quickly quote from the book of Deuteronomy was a key to Satan's defeat.

Scripture memorization is one of the most urgently needed disciplines of the Christian home and the Christian church. If we are not equipping ourselves for battle by memorizing the Word, our best weapon will be just out of our reach when we most need it. Satan is waiting to find "an opportune time" in each of our lives. That opportune time will arise when we have no Bible nearby, and our weapon will be out of reach if we do not have it memorized.

There are many ways to memorize. Some can memorize large sections of the Word by simply reading them many times. For many years, when calling on hospital patients, I read favorite passages of the Word that spoke of the Lord's comfort. One day, having left my Bible in the car, I discovered to my surprise that I could quote those portions almost perfectly. Others find it helpful to write out verses or paragraphs on cards to carry with them, then work on memorizing them in spare moments. It is helpful to work with another person when memorizing, so you can check on each other. Most people work more effectively under the principle of accountability.

It is equally important that you correctly understand the Word of God. One who memorizes the Word must also be one who "correctly handles the word of truth" (2 Timothy 2:15). When Satan quoted the Scriptures to Jesus during His temptation, he misinterpreted them. That is one of Satan's most clever tricks. He wants us to misunderstand the Word or misuse it. Some of the most effective human instruments Satan has are people who use the Bible effusively, but incorrectly.

When memorizing the Word of God, it is effective to express in your own words what the text is saying. If you have any doubt about the meaning, use a trustworthy Bible commentary to arrive at a correct understanding.

Satan may use a wrong understanding of a passage of Scripture to paralyze a Christian's effectiveness. I one day had a call from a Christian lady who was in severe distress. She was the wife of a prominent physician in a distant city and very active in a Bible-preaching church. She had got into a great deal of difficulty over two passages of Scripture in the book of Hebrews (6:4-6; 10:26-31). Satan kept tormenting her into believing that she had "fallen away" and that she had lost her salvation and could not be saved again. In trying to help, I asked her if she had ever prayed over those passages, repeatedly read them, and sought to understand what they really said. "Oh, no," was her reply "They always frighten me too much, and I try not to read them."

Her response was typical of how Satan tries to misuse the Word of God. By tormenting her, the enemy was able to keep her from mastering the Word. I urged her to make an exhaustive study of those passages. Admittedly, they are some of the most difficult texts to understand, and I assured her that she would find good Bible scholars differing in their approach to those texts. Yet, the Word is the truth of God, and God wants us to know it.

We must know the Scripture and insist that the enemy acknowledge our stand. We can only do this effectively as we build our lives upon God's Word, "rooted and grounded" in the truth. We cannot build effective warfare upon anything else. Feelings will not do. Feelings are as changeable as the wind. Our own discipline and dedication will not do. One day we are up, and another day we are down. Only the Word of God effectively dispatches the enemy.

Satan will not easily back off from you even when you use the Word against him. He will test you and try to get you to doubt the truth of the Word. He will challenge you. It is always important to establish your authority over him because of your union with Christ. The enemy may deny that Christ has authority over him. But if you know the Word and quote the Word, establishing Christ's authority, you can always force him to admit that Christ has authority over all principalities and powers (Ephesians 1:19-22; Philippians 2:9-11).

The Person of the Spirit

We must not fail to recognize that behind "the sword of the Spirit" is a Person, the Holy Spirit. He is the one who makes our sword effective in battle.

Peter's experience in the garden when men came to take Jesus is an example of a believer's swinging the wrong sword (John 18:10). He used the wrong sword and was trusting in the wrong strength to be effective in battle. The only result was that Malchus lost an ear. If our Lord had not been there to heal the ear immediately, not only would Malchus have suffered injury, but the entire company of disciples could have been arrested, perhaps imprisoned, or even crucified with Jesus. Our Lord often has to rescue us when we go about swinging the wrong sword in spiritual battle. Later that same man, Peter, swung the sword of the Spirit on the day of Pentecost. Instead of injuring one man's ear, he captured and spiritually healed three thousand "ears." Three thousand people responded to the Word of salvation and were baptized as believers.

We cannot effectively use the Word of God in warfare unless the Holy Spirit is controlling us. "But the fruit of the Spirit is love, joy, peace, patience, kindness, goodness, faithfulness, gentleness and self-control. Against such things there is no law" (Galatians 5:22-23). We cannot fight spiritual battles in a fleshly way.

In the early years of my ministry, a member of the church I pastored was very difficult to work with. She had a sharp tongue, a quick temper, and she was somewhat overbearing. Through the years she had offended many people. It would have been fairly easy to have voted her out of the church, as some of the deacons wanted to do. After a couple of sharp encounters with her myself, I felt that might not be a bad idea. I went so far as to pray about it. Afterward, I remember thinking, *If I do that, God will give me two more just like her.* God had put her there for me to love, to nurture, to train, to feed, and to lead, not to kick out. How often we get into trouble when we resort to a method other than that "of the spirit." Satan moves in on such situations even when we feel we are right and the other person is wrong. He indeed may be very wrong, but we can never do good things in a fleshly way.

We must also remember not to resist the Holy Spirit in one area of life while trying to use the "sword of the Spirit" in another. Several years ago, a woman who was under severe assault from the powers of darkness came to me for counseling. I used all the methods of warfare I knew but was still not very successful. After several weeks of counseling, I could see no improvement. She was memorizing the Word, practicing aggressive resistance of the enemy, praying doctrinally-oriented prayers, but still seemed to be losing the battle. I finally concluded something was seriously wrong.

In kindness, I asked her if she was resisting the Holy Spirit in some area. She hung her head and finally told me she had a smoking problem. She did not smoke heavily, but she was aware that it was a habit she would not submit to the Holy Spirit. We dealt with that, and immediate improvement began. The intensity of the battle subsided, and the last I knew, she was walking tall in victory.

It is the Holy Spirit who applies the power of the "sword" against our foe. If we are grieving or quenching His work in our lives in any area, Satan will be quick to take advantage of that opening.

All spiritual victory is essentially bound to the Word of God. Satan retreats as the Word of God, the sword of the Spirit, is used against him.

Taking Up the Sword

In the name of the Lord Jesus Christ, I lay hold of the sword of the Spirit, the Word of God. I embrace its inerrant message of truth and power. I humbly ask the Holy Spirit to guide me into true understanding of the message of the Word. Grant to me the discipline and dedication to memorize the Word and to saturate my mind with its truth and power.

In the name of the Lord Jesus Christ and by the ministry of the Holy Spirit, grant to me the wisdom to always apply the Word against the enemy. May I use the Word to defeat Satan and to advance the cause of Christ into that very realm Satan claims. Amen.

11

The Allness of Prayer

> And pray in the Spirit on all occasions with all kinds of prayers and requests. With this in mind, be alert and always keep on praying for all the saints. (Ephesians 6:18)

That verse helps to convey the *all*-importance of prayer in one's being invincible to do the will of God. Four times the concept of "allness" is presented. Prayer is not simply an additional part of the believer's armor, but rather is of equal importance to the armor.

We have covered the four keys to victory as set forth in Ephesians 6:10-18. The first is the believer's position and relationship to Christ. "Finally, be strong in the Lord" (Ephesians 6:10*a*). The believer's inseparable union with Christ in all His Person and work makes him invincible.

The second key is the work and ministry of the Holy Spirit. "Be strong . . . in his mighty power" (Ephesians 6:10*b*). We are able to enjoy and experience "his mighty power," only as the Holy Spirit fills and empowers us (Acts 1:8; Ephesians 3:16).

The third key is the whole armor of God (Ephesians 6:11-17). As we carefully clothe ourselves with that spiritual clothing, we become a formidable opponent to the powers of darkness. We have given careful consideration to each part of the armor, stressing the importance of claiming it by faith.

The fourth key to victory, however, is critical. None of us will be successful in spiritual warfare without prayer. The apostle Paul repeatedly calls our attention to the importance of prayer in the book of Ephesians. In Ephesians 1:15-23, Paul reveals the intensity of his own prayers for the Ephesian believers. Warren Wiersbe points out that in this prayer "he does not ask God to give them what they do not have, but rather prays that God will reveal to them what they already have."[1]

In Ephesians 3:14-21, Paul presents a picture of himself bowing in prayer before the heavenly Father. He prays that the Ephesians might be enabled to do God's will. The burden of his prayer is that those believers might lay hold of the "glorious riches" available in Christ (Ephesians 3:16), which are "immeasurably more than all we ask or imagine" (Ephesians 3:20). Through those riches we are able to be energized by the power of the Spirit and to enjoy "the fullness of God" (Ephesians 3:19). Prayer is the key to *enlightenment* and *enablement* in enjoying the "glorious riches" of God.

The Preeminence of Prayer

In Ephesians 6:18, Paul admonishes us to pray "on all occasions," or "in all seasons." That means to pray when you feel like it and when you don't feel like it. The preeminence of prayer needs to be firmly settled in our minds. There is no place for half-hearted, passive involvement when it comes to warfare praying.

A. T. Pierson wrote: "Every new Pentecost has had its preparatory period of supplement—of waiting for enduement; and sometimes the time of tarrying has been lengthened from 'ten days' to as many weeks, months, or even years; but never has there been an outpouring of the Divine Spirit from God without a previous outpouring of the human spirit toward God. To vindicate this statement would require us to trace the whole history of missions, for the field of such display of divine power covers the ages. Yet every missionary biography, from those of Elliot and Edwards, Brainerd and Carey, down to Livingstone and Burns, Hudson Taylor and John E. Clough, tells the same story: prayer has been the preparation for every new triumph; and so, if greater triumphs and successes lie before us, more fervent and faithful praying must be their forerunner and herald!"[2]

It is impossible to overemphasize the role of biblical prayer in the victory of believers.

The Passion of Prayer

We are to pray "with all kinds of prayers and requests." Have you ever considered how many different kinds of prayers there are? There

1. Warren Wiersbe, *Be Rich* (Wheaton, Ill.: Scripture Press, 1976), 30.
2. Charles Cook, ed., *Daily Meditations for Prayer* (Westchester, Ill.: Good News Publishers, n.d.), 27.

is silent prayer and audible prayer, prayer without ceasing and prayer that terminates, public prayer and private prayer, short prayer and extended prayer, fasting prayer and feasting prayer, prayer with one's life and prayer with one's words, rejoicing prayer and broken prayer, thanksgiving prayer and asking prayer, doctrinal prayer and emotional prayer, resisting-the-enemy prayer and standing-with-the-Lord prayer. There are probably other kinds of prayers we could consider, but the truth is that all kinds of prayers are a part of our warfare.

At times it is important just to praise the Lord in prayer. I recall an occasion when a distraught husband brought his troubled wife to counsel with me. She was under severe affliction from demonic powers. Although she did not know where our house was, the powers of darkness afflicting her did. As they neared our home, she began to scream uncontrollably and tried to jump out of the moving car. With considerable difficulty, the husband was able to steer her through our door and into a private counseling room. There she was like a frightened, caged animal, trying to flee, only to be blocked by her husband. When I could gain no communication with her, the Holy Spirit led me to praise the Lord in prayer and song. I began to pray a doctrinal prayer of praise, enumerating the wondrous attributes of God and describing what it means to abide in Christ. At first there seemed to be a violent reaction from the powers of darkness afflicting her. But as the praise continued, Satan's power was broken, and she became calm as the "peace of God" settled upon her.

Resisting the enemy in prayer is something we do not employ as often as we should. "For though we live in the world, we do not wage war as the world does. The weapons we fight with are not the weapons of the world. On the contrary, they have divine power to demolish strongholds" (2 Corinthians 10:3-4). What a challenge that verse is to us—that we would see our "divine power" to resist the strategies of Satan. Joshua and the people of Israel achieved the same kind of victory against Jericho. The walls of the enemy were so thick and strong that there seemed to be no way Israel could take that mighty city. Yet by prayer and obedience to the Word of the Lord, the walls fell. They didn't even throw a stone. That is the way it is in spiritual warfare. Impossible fortifications crumble into dust before the believer who uses the divine power of his weapons to pull down strongholds. Like Israel, we can then walk through the gates and plunder the enemy's land.

Do you schedule an hour or two with God several times each week? Martin Luther did so the first two hours of every day. Spurgeon had shut-away times when it was said not even a visit from the King of England would cause him to interrupt his prayer.

The Greek word translated "supplication" means, literally, "the character of necessity or compulsion in prayer." To bind yourself to the Lord with such a tie of petition is to insure the answer. Every prayer has an answer, even if it is "No" or "Wait."

The Paraclete of Prayer

We are to pray "in the Spirit." Some would interpret this to mean that we must pray in "tongues." The Bible indicates otherwise. Paul's prayers in Ephesians 1 and 3 were certainly "in the Spirit" and were not uttered in "tongues."

I give a word of warning to those who seek to "pray in tongues." To those who have shared their experiences with me, I ask, "Have you tested the spirit authoring your 'tongue'? The Holy Spirit Himself tells us to do that in 1 John 4:1-4. While a person prays in a "tongue," his own mind is largely in a neutral state. I suggest that he command the spirit authoring the tongue to answer clearly in his mind, "Has Jesus Christ come in the flesh? Is Jesus Christ Lord? Do you honor the blood of Jesus Christ?" Insist upon a clear and precise answer. The Holy Spirit will always answer with rejoicing "Yes!" Another spirit will be evasive or even on some occasions give a blatant "No." It is important to avoid being deceived by a "lying spirit," lest Satan gain an advantage against us.

Praying in the Spirit means praying in harmony with the Spirit or under the control of the Spirit. Several practical steps will insure that we are praying in the Spirit. First, we must ask the Holy Spirit to control our praying and to guide us to pray in harmony with His will. That is one of the Holy Spirit's ministries according to Romans 8:26-27: "In the same way, the Spirit helps us in our weakness. We do not know what we ought to pray, but the Spirit himself intercedes for us with groans that words cannot express. And he who searches our hearts knows the mind of the Spirit, because the Spirit intercedes for the saints in accordance with God's will."

We also need to deliberately reject all fleshly praying. James warns, "When you ask, you do not receive, because you ask with wrong motives, that you may spend what you get on your pleasures" (James 4:3). It is good to say as one begins to pray, "In the name of the Lord Jesus Christ I reject the involvement of my old sin nature in my prayer. I count myself dead with Christ to my sin nature and its control, and I ask the Holy Spirit to sovereignly oversee the words of my prayer."

A third suggestion is to pray in harmony with the truth of the Word. The Word of God is Holy Spirit breathed (2 Timothy 3:16-17).

When we pray God's Word back to Him, we can be sure that we pray in the Spirit. Memorizing prayers from the Psalms or other great prayers of the Bible is a way to be sure of praying in the Spirit. One can certainly pray in the Spirit if he prays a prayer like Paul's prayer for the Ephesian believers in Ephesians 3:14-21. It is good to master such passages in order to know how to pray for yourself and your church. Matthew 6:9-13, the "Lord's Prayer," can serve as a good guideline for praying in the Spirit.

Probably all of us have experienced times of prayer when the words flowed easily and the heart was warm toward God. Sometimes we interpret those prayers as being in the Spirit, whereas difficult times are regarded as not being so. Yet, many of the prayers recorded in the Psalms begin with the lament that God seems far off and silent (see Psalms 28, 55, 102).

For a number of years, I sensed barriers and walls during shut-away times of in-depth prayer. How glad I was to realize that such times of prayer can also be in the Spirit. The deep emotion of such times often teach us more and express our needs more effectively than times of greater liberty do. Doctrinal praying—praying the truth of God's Word back to Him—will aid in breaking through the times when barriers seem to hide God's face from us.

The Protection of Prayer

"With this in mind, be alert." This phrase has a military ring to it. It conveys the picture of a sentry on duty, guarding something that needs protection. In spiritual warfare, the believer must stand guard through prayer, watching over himself, his family, his church, and the work of the Lord.

In the military, someone on sentry duty is there to prevent surprise attack from unseen enemies. When she was still living, my wife's mother always included in her prayers the words "Protect us from dangers and enemies, seen and unseen." She was "being alert," and everytime I heard her pray that way it always impressed me. Who can know what terrible calamities are avoided by alert praying.

The Lord Jesus employed that kind of warfare praying. To Peter the Lord Jesus said, "Simon, Simon, Satan has asked to sift you as wheat. But I have prayed for you, Simon, that your faith may not fail. And when you have turned back, strengthen your brothers" (Luke 22:31-32). Christ was being alert for Peter and the other apostles. The same kind of "sentry duty" prayer is evidenced in His great high priestly prayer of John 17.

I learned of a missionary who returned home from the field discouraged and broken-hearted, when two of her older children attending school in this country were showing signs of serious rebellion against all that they had been taught and professed to believe. Having always prayed for her children, she was in a quandary about what to do. Someone gave her a copy of *The Adversary,* and she took up the challenge of warfare praying with fervency. She later called me and shared that prayer had dramatically turned around the lives of her children. She returned to the field with a new awareness of her responsibility to be alert for her family.

Satan would like nothing better than to harm us. He would afflict us with illness, misfortune, or misery if he had but one opportunity. When employing protective warfare praying, we can watch for ways that the Lord protects us.

One Saturday morning, my wife and I were driving home in separate cars from an early morning prayer meeting at our church. While I watched in my rearview mirror to see that my wife was following me, she arrived at an intersection just as a careless driver, traveling much too fast, sped through, barely missing her car. For a moment, it seemed certain that an accident would occur. Yet, as I viewed the whole thing in my rearview mirror, restful assurance flooded my soul. That very morning I had carefully watched over my entire family in warfare prayer. Guardian angels and a sovereign, protecting Shepherd were on duty in answer to prayer. Just another near miss? No, I'm certain it wasn't.

The Perseverance of Prayer

There is no more important word than *persistence* in warfare praying. We need to claim daily our union with Christ, appropriate the Holy Spirit's work, put on each part of the armor, and employ persistent prayer. Many times a day we may be called upon to use those elements in our efforts to win the battle. We must be persistent. We must not let down if things are going well and suppose such faithful warfare is not necessary.

A man shared with me his problem with lust and pornography. We considered carefully the steps to overcoming the lusts of the flesh. First, we talked about the need to be honest and admit to oneself and to God that the old sin nature was at work. Then we went over the need to reckon oneself dead with Christ to the rule and reign of that sin (Romans 6:11). We can by faith affirm that to be true, because it is true. We are responsible to "not let sin reign in [our] mortal bod[ies]" (Romans 6:12). The only way we can do that is to recognize that we have been crucified with Christ (Galatians 2:20). Third, we discussed the need to ask the Holy Spirit to replace our fleshly, sinful desires with the fruit of the Spirit: "love, joy, peace, patience, kindness, goodness, faithfulness, gentleness, and self-control" (Galatians 5:22-23).

We went over those three steps until he could repeat them back to me, and he promised to use them each time he came under temptation.

A few weeks later he came into my study, slumped in a chair, and groaned about being defeated by the lusts of the flesh. I listened attentively and sympathetically for a time, but then I asked him, "What are the biblical steps to overcoming your sin nature?" He was stumped. He remembered we had talked about that previously, but he couldn't recall what the three steps were.

Once again we went over them. I showed him carefully that each of those three steps is set forth as God's way to victory over the flesh. I kept encouraging him until he could repeat them back to me. I then told him that until he put those steps into consistent practice, I could do no more for him. Even God could do nothing more for him until he began to use what had already been provided.

We must also be *insistent.* It would be much easier if our enemy were willing to admit that we have full authority over him because we are united with Christ in all of His victory. Yet, he is not that kind of enemy. He but grudgingly admits such victory. Most of us have observed a disobedient child reluctantly giving in to the authority of his parent. He doesn't give an inch until he just has to. Satan and his demons are like that. This is why in warfare our prayer needs to be insistent in our persistence. There are times in all of our lives when everything seems to be failing and the enemy seems to be winning at every turn. That is the very time we need to be most insistent that he just can't win.

In Acts 16, Paul and Silas successfully cast out a demon from a young fortune-teller. Those who made money from her fortune-telling had Paul and Silas arrested, roughly handled, and finally put in a dungeon, locked up in stocks. That pictures Satan's refusal to admit he is defeated. Instead of feeling sorry for themselves and complaining about how the devil was beating them, they prayed and sang songs of victory. The other prisoners all heard them at midnight. In faith and practice, despite outward evidence to the contrary, they just kept insisting on their victory. Suddenly the prison shook, their stocks fell off, the doors opened, and they were free. The victory went on to such dimension that the jailer and his family were saved, and the town authorities who had treated them so badly had to apologize (see Acts 16). Truth must win. Persistence faces all tests and just keeps on insisting that evil must yield to truth.

The Panorama of Prayer

Warfare prayer is to be "for all the saints." Does that take your breath away as it did mine the first time I saw it? What a vast spectrum of responsibility we have in warfare praying. It can be viewed as an ever-widening series of circles extending outward. Your first responsibility is for yourself. Each believer has the care of his own life and ministry to oversee. The next step out is your family. No one will watch over your family in prayer as you will. The circles then extend to your church, your denomination, your missionaries, and the entire Body of Christ around the world. Christ commanded the disciples to witness to Jerusalem, Judea, Samaria, and the uttermost parts of the earth. "For all saints" prayer reaches out that far, too. It has a panorama of responsibility that embraces the whole world.

Since being on a preaching mission to Britain in 1964, I have felt a special prayer responsibility for that nation. Many times as I have wrestled in prayer for the believers there and for revival in Britain, the Holy Spirit has broken my heart to tears for that nation. Others have felt the same concern for China.

The Projection of Prayer

In Ephesians 6:18 we see that prayer should be projected to "all the saints." In verses 19 and 20 we see that warfare prayer can specifically be projected toward the effectiveness of our ministry.

Paul asks the Ephesians: "Pray also for me, that whenever I open my mouth, words may be given" (Ephesians 6:19). He is saying that the warfare prayer of the Ephesian believers can enable him to have greater ability to communicate the gospel. Every preacher knows the truth of those words. All of us have had the experience of studying hard and preparing diligently, only to try to deliver the message and find the words will not come. My wife has developed a capacity to know when I am facing such a trial. I have often seen her bow her head in prayer to ask that "words may be given." And often the barriers have been broken on such occasions.

That kind of prayer also effects boldness in proclaiming the gospel. Paul says their prayers for him will enable him to "fearlessly make known the mystery of the gospel" (Ephesians 6:19). We not only need to pray for fearless preaching, but we need to pray for open ears.

Prayer directly affects how people hear the Word. That is why prayer support for revival crusades can help bring many souls to Christ. It helps to remove the spiritual blindness and deafness that Satan wants to perpetuate (see 2 Corinthians 4:4). There is no force in the hands of man as effective and far-reaching as prayer. A person of God can literally change the world through his prayers without leaving the confines of his own home.

From the journal of David Brainerd comes this insight: "In the afternoon God was with me of a truth. Oh, it was blessed company indeed! God enabled me so to agonize in prayer that I was quite wet with sweat, though in the shade and cool wind. My soul was drawn out very much for the world; I grasped for multitudes of souls. I think I had more enlargement for sinners than for the children of God, though I felt as if I could spend my life in cries for both. I had great joy in communion with my dear Saviour. I think I never in my life felt such an entire weanedness from this world, and so much resigned to God in everything. Oh, that I may always live to and upon my blessed God! Amen."[3]

Those are the words of a man who knew something of the all-that verse is as far-reaching as God Himself. Paul seems deliberately to leave the challenge open-ended. To be able through prayer to touch and minister to "all the saints" is beyond our comprehension. The invincible power of prayer knows no bounds.

3. Ibid., 310.

12

Invincible Prayer in Action

My mother was born on a farm in Iowa shortly after her parents emigrated from Scotland. She knew what it was to work hard and stretch meager funds to meet the many demands of life. Poverty did not dull her spirit, though, and eventually better times came into her life. She married a prosperous young farmer. He built a spacious new home with many of the modern conveniences other farm homes did not have. They were blessed with three healthy sons, and that kept her busy but happy and fulfilled. The farm did well, and the future seemed bright with promise. She came to know Christ as her Savior, and after her conversion, God's blessings seemed to have no end. All seemed right with her world.

Then, like a sudden storm unleashing its fury, heartbreaking disappointment fell upon her. One heartache mounted on top of another. During the Great Depression, my father lost one farm and was in danger of losing our home. In the midst of financial trial, Mother gave birth to her first and only daughter, a beautiful baby with a serious birth defect, who lived only three days. The beloved church where Mother had found Christ closed its doors, and the building was sold. Then, illness added its burden. Her youngest son went from one siege of double pneumonia into another, and as the doctor left the house one day, he said, "He cannot live through the night."

Heartbroken, frightened, and desperate, her overwhelming needs closed in upon her. What could she do? Who could help? She had no pastor to call. Even family and Christian friends were not near at hand.

Overwhelmed, she fled to her room and fell to her knees. My father joined her in prayer for a time, but sleep eventually overtook him. She could not sleep, however. She kept praying, shut in with God for most of the night. In the midst of prayer, a method of treating her son's pneumonia came to her mind. She felt the idea for treatment to be a leading from the Lord. She applied it, and her son's life was saved. Courage and faith were born anew in her heart. Perhaps of more importance, in that moment of need she learned a greatness in prayer that continued to characterize her life until the time of her death.

I was that son who was healed of pneumonia. I have many beautiful memories of that noble woman who was my mother, but the crowning memory is the greatness and power of her prayer life. How very fortunate is that person who, when surrounded by overwhelming trials and burdens, learns to pray. It took me many years to learn that myself.

Learning to Pray

When I began preparation for the ministry at the Moody Bible Institute in Chicago, one of my first assignments was Sunday visitation at the huge Cook County Hospital. A group of us would station ourselves at the hospital entrances, ready to hand out gospel tracts as visitors arrived. I disliked that part of the assignment. People in a hurry to visit loved ones seemed in no mood to be stopped and handed a tract. Some would refuse them; others would crumple them and throw them away. The withering looks of contempt and muttered oaths of disgust I received soon reduced a meek boy from the country into a hiding missionary. I would find a convenient pillar and hide behind it, remaining as much out of the line of traffic as I could. I sincerely hoped no one would come my way, stirring my conscience to hand him a tract.

One Sunday, I was in my favorite hiding place, eagerly waiting for the time I could go to the wards and visit with patients. I looked across the lobby and saw a black man handing out tracts. His face was radiant. It seemed to shine with an inner light. His voice was quiet, but its resonant tone reached me across the lobby.

"God bless you, brother. Here's something that will cheer your day."

"Jesus loves you, my friend."

"Isn't it wonderful to know there is a hope beyond our troubles?"

As he handed out the tracts and spoke words of kindness, something amazing happened. People stopped. They took the tracts. Some walked a few steps, stopped, and began to read. Others took the tracts and with what seemed like deliberate reverence, put them into a pocket or purse. I felt sure they intended to read the message later. Even those who refused tracts seemed to walk on with a shamed look.

Others would stop and just look at the man. They seemed captivated by the outflow of his love, arrested by the glow of his goodness.

My interest was aroused. I guess I was a little stunned. What accounted for the remarkable contrast between the way people received the tracts from this man and from me? Where did his radiance come from? Why did that quiet voice have such a ring of compelling authority?

Later I learned that radiant man was Chaplain Lilly. He had a full-time ministry at the hospital, visiting lonely patients and sharing Christ with them. His ministry of love included carrying a shaving kit and barber tools, and he even offered to trim the toenails of patients who lingered many months in the hospital. His words and deeds of love combined to bring many to saving faith in Jesus Christ. I longed to know his secret.

It was on the closing Sunday of that assignment that God privileged me to see the answer. Our assignment leader took us on a tour of the hospital. I remember little of that tour except the little "hole in the wall" that was Chaplain Lilly's "office." In one corner was a large overstuffed chair draped with a white sheet. Pointing to the chair, our tour leader said, "That's Chaplain Lilly's throne chair. He never just sits in that chair. Before he goes up to the wards to visit, he often spends hours in prayer for his sick friends and for God's blessing on his ministry."

That's it! I thought. Immediately I knew what accounted for his radiance and the difference in people's response to him. It was prayer.

That was one of the greatest lessons God ever taught me. It still lingers in my soul like a special fragrance of grace. One thing will always mark a person who has both power with men and power with God. He will be a man who is great in prayer. Each significant movement toward God in the spiritual affairs of men will be preceded and accompanied by greatness of prayer. "The prayer of a righteous man is powerful and effective" (James 5:16).

Moving God to Action

Great prayers get answers. Sometimes all it takes is one person to put God's plan in motion. Armin Gesswein relates the history of a revival that visited Norway in the early 1930s and lasted until the tragic Nazi invasion of that country. For nearly a decade, the awakening moved in numerous churches. As a result, more than 20,000 souls found Christ as Savior and Lord. It was under the preaching of Frank Mangs, an evangelist from Sweden, that the revival spread rapidly to many churches of Norway. He preached for two years, scarcely daring to leave because of the mighty way the Spirit of God was moving. Even after that initial move, he kept returning to preach, and no building would hold the number of people who wanted to hear the Word of God.

Actually, the work of revival had begun some time before Frank Mangs appeared on the scene, in the Betlehem Church in Oslo. The church's prayer meeting had reached such a low point that Pastor Ludvig Johnson was considering giving it up. His faithful wife encouraged him by saying, "Dear, we'll keep the prayer meeting even if you and I are the only ones who go." God honored that faith.

But the real secret went back even farther—to the church sexton, a very humble man with faith in the invincible power of prayer. He had been disturbed for some time by the coldness of the church and the obvious worldliness of so many of its members. The sermons seemed dry and dull. Attendance waned, and enthusiasm for prayer and the things of God was at a low ebb. The sexton asked God what he could do about it. His heart leaped with excitement as by faith he felt a challenge from the Lord. Early in the mornings before he began his duties, he would make his way up behind the pulpit. There he knelt and pleaded for God to revive his heart, his pastor, and the entire church. Holy tears often anointed the carpet as he bent his face low before God in Spirit-led prayer. So sure was this humble servant of God that his prayers would prevail that shortly after the new year he took the assistant pastor, Holm-Glad, up to the pulpit of the church when no one else was present. He pointed to the empty seats of the church and said, "There is going to be a revival here this year." Holm-Glad said later that he almost laughed because there seemed to be no sign of anything like that. The caretaker, while not sharing his secret of prayer, reaffirmed his certainty that revival would come that year.

Weeks passed, then months, and changes began to appear. The pastor's message began to ring with a new authority and flowed from a heart warmed toward God. The prayer meetings began to grow, and crowds began to attend the services. Finally the outbreak of God's Spirit through the preaching of Frank Mangs not only touched that church but all of Oslo and large areas of Norway.

A year after the revival had broken out, Betlehem Church had a meeting to celebrate the great work of God with a festive dinner followed by a praise service. After the service, the sexton took Pastor Holm-Glad into the sanctuary. With humble tears he said, "Do you remember how I told you there would be a revival here?"

"How could I forget?" responded Holm-Glad.

"Now I am free to tell you how I knew," said the sexton. "Only God knows how many times He burdened my heart to kneel behind the pulpit in prayer for revival. How often I wept sore before the Lord behind this pulpit. We are celebrating today, and God laid it on my heart to tell you this."

I'm so thankful that God burdened that humble, behind-the-scenes servant of the Lord to share that story. How much richer we are to see the invincible power of prayer through any servant who dares to see his invincible position. Great prayer causes God to visibly move in the affairs of men.

Acts 12 records Peter's arrest and imprisonment by Herod. He was scheduled to be tried and probably executed. "But the church was earnestly praying to God for him" (Acts 12:5).

Those prayers brought God into action. An angel left heaven's glory to interfere in the plans of the enemy. The chains that bound Peter to his guards fell off, and the light of heaven flooded his dungeon. As he wrapped his garments about him and followed the angel, the prison sentries could not even see Peter. Locked iron gates seemed to come alive and opened at the bidding of heaven's royalty. Unbound and free, Peter went to the prayer meeting, where astonished prayer servants witnessed the living answer to their petitions. God's dramatic, visible movings in response to great prayer stirred a church and defeated the enemy.

Entering into the Burden

A study of the book of Nehemiah will reveal a striking illustration of greatness in prayer. Nehemiah was in exile in Persia and was serving as cupbearer to the king. As he heard an eyewitness account of the deplorable state of Jerusalem, the tragedy of that great city with broken walls and burned gates broke his heart. Accounts of his Hebrew brethren being greatly afflicted aroused his empathy and moved his soul. Nehemiah was living as a captive in a foreign land, yet he was much better off than those who had escaped capture and stayed in Jerusalem. It was in that hour that he began to pray. He spent many days in tears, fasting, and praying, mourning over the victories God's enemies were having in Jerusalem. The urgency of the need drove him into a greatness of prayer seldom seen among men.

There is no lack of needs around today, but few seem to take the responsibility for them that Nehemiah felt. Not all believers seem to have the capacity to see need. But even of those who do, only a few seem to let that need take them to the place of greatness in prayer. Some turn away from prayer at such times with the thought *What's the use anyway? What can I do about it?* Yet, in times of great need, prompt action in faithful prayer can change the course of events.

Sometimes we are not even prepared to devote time and energy to prayer for our own burdens. A woman called me long distance to seek my counsel about her battle with Satan. She insisted that she needed instant deliverance. "I don't want to practice all of this warfare bit. I want you to command Satan to leave me. I want to be done with this battle immediately like Jesus set the man from Gadara free." I have heard similar statements many times from those battling with Satan's kingdom. People want push-button deliverance. We are the product of our age. In this day of instant soup and immediate computer printouts, we don't want to wait for an answer or carry a burden—even the burden of the Lord.

There is nothing wrong with having a burden so great we must express ourselves in tears, fasting, and extended prayer. Such a burden can be a vital part of living out God's plan. When you experience such a burden, it is good to remember the wise words of an elderly but unlearned man of God. When asked what Scripture passage was his favorite, he admitted that he liked best the words "and it came to pass." Asked why those words were his favorite, he replied, "Well, it's this way. Whenever I read those blessed words 'and it came to pass,' I know that my burdens and troubles ain't come to stay, they's come to pass."

It's obvious that emotionally we could not always carry a burden as heavy as Nehemiah's on our hearts. God knows that and will see us through to victory in ample time to accomplish His plan. Great needs are meant to bring Christians to their knees in great prayer and ultimately to bring spiritual advancement.

Expecting the Victory

One night after midnight, our doorbell rang. I put on my robe and hurried to answer it. Peering through the window in the door, I could see a man I knew standing in the cold in his bare feet and dressed only in his pajamas. As I opened the door, he fairly rushed into my arms, pleading for me to help him. I ushered him into a room where we could talk and learned that he felt under attack from the powers of darkness. As a professing Christian, he had been going through some severe trials. On that night, he had awakened with the terrifying sense that some evil powers were trying to take over his being and even kill him.

I began to pray for him, and as I prayed he was seized by some convulsive force that seemed literally to throw him upon the floor. I continued to pray, quoting the Word of God and focusing the victory of Christ upon the man, sometimes commanding any powers of darkness tormenting him to leave him and go where Jesus Christ would send them.

As I continued praying that way, he began to gesture threateningly at me. He was large enough and strong enough to have doubtlessly overpowered me, had he been able to proceed with his threats. I continued to address the promises of the Word against the forces of Satan. As he came toward me, I quoted 1 John 5:18, "He that is begotten of God keepeth himself, and that wicked one toucheth him not" (KJV) and 1 John 3:8, "The Son of God was manifested, that he might destroy the works of the devil" (KJV). Several times he seemed almost violently thrown back from me. Finally, the war was won. He was calm and able to pray himself and thank the Lord for the victory. He later told me that he seemed controlled by a violent power that strongly wanted to hurt me. Yet each time I addressed the Word of God against the power of darkness seeking to control him, it was as though that violent force was hurled away from me by some invincible power. The Word of God is invincible when rightly understood and applied.

Invincible prayer is centered in great expectancy. Nehemiah expected God to so touch the heart of a pagan king that he would be favorable to rebuilding a walled city that had been destroyed by war. He expected God to incline the king's heart to put him, a lowly cup bearer, in charge of a great expedition to return to Jerusalem to rebuild the walls. Nehemiah expected the Jews in Jerusalem to respond and help him. He expected that the enemies who would oppose the task would be defeated. He expected a government to be reestablished in Jerusalem and the economy to be rebuilt. In short, he expected God to accomplish His will for His people.

And Nehemiah accomplished all that he expected to and more. God kept enlarging his expectancy as he moved from victory to victory. The walls were rebuilt. Enemies were defeated. The gates were hung, and city government and worship were reestablished. Confident expectancy is an essential part of the invincible, victorious walk. As His children, we can expect God to accomplish through every one of us His will and purpose for our lives.

Taking an Invincible Stance

Gracious heavenly Father, I choose to see myself as You see me in the Person of Your Son, the Lord Jesus Christ. I choose to see myself as one invincibly strong and able to do all that is in Your will for me to do. I reject Satan's accusations that I am hopelessly weak and defeated. I accept my present great need as a call to renewed vision of the victory of my Lord. Help me to focus my attention upon the awesome majesty, power, and sovereign greatness of my heavenly Father, who can do anything but fail. Help me to see that in my union with Christ I am more than a conqueror. Let the burden of my trials become an expression of the burden of the Lord. Let that burden be expressed in tears of concern, times of fasting and prayer. I choose not to shrink back from the burden You wish me to carry.

I recognize, Lord, that it is chiefly my own sin and failure that has brought me to this severe trial. I am deeply sorry for my sins. [Mention them by name.] Cleanse me in my Savior's blood. I take back from Satan all ground I have given him by my sins and transgressions. On the authority of the cross I reclaim all of that ground for the Lord Jesus Christ.

Precious Lord Jesus Christ, You have promised never to leave me nor forsake me. I know that is true, and I boldly say, "The Lord is my helper, I will not fear." I resist the devil and his kingdom, steadfast in the faith. I command Satan and his demons to leave me and to go where the Lord Jesus Christ sends them.

Heavenly Father, I accept and choose to enjoy everything inscribed upon the scroll of Your will for me. Thank You that I can do all things through Christ who is my strength. I will do Your will by accepting my responsibility to be strong. I will do through Your strength the things I know to be Your will. [Tell Him what they are.]

Thank You, loving heavenly Father, that through my Lord Jesus Christ You have heard my prayer—and You will make me to walk as one so strong in the Lord that even Satan's most powerful strategies are already defeated. In the name of the Lord Jesus Christ and for Your glory I pray. Amen.

Epilogue: Nothing but a Winner

> To him who is able to keep you from falling and to present you before His glorious presence without fault and with great joy—to the only God our Savior be glory, majesty, power and authority, through Jesus Christ our Lord, before all ages, now and forevermore! Amen. (Jude 24-25)
>
> May God himself, the God of peace, sanctify you through and through. May your whole spirit, soul and body be kept blameless at the coming of our Lord Jesus Christ. The one who calls you is faithful and he will do it. (1 Thessalonians 5:23-24)
>
> May the God of peace, who through the blood of the eternal covenant brought back from the dead our Lord Jesus, that great Shepherd of the sheep, equip you with everything good for doing his will, and may he work in us what is pleasing to him, through Jesus Christ, to whom be glory for ever and ever. Amen. (Hebrews 13:20-21)
>
> Now to him who is able to do immeasurably more than all we ask or imagine, according to his power that is at work within us, to him be glory in the church and in Christ Jesus throughout all generations, for ever and ever! Amen. (Ephesians 3:20-21)

Each of those passages is what the church has come to call a benediction, a pronouncement of blessing. Benedictions usually contain summations of great truth designed to comfort, assure, and promote confidence in the hearts of God's people. Those quoted here certainly do that. I would recommend each of them for the reader's memorization and meditation. They assure us that as God's own we are destined to be winners because of the victory Christ has won.

I would like this brief closing to be a kind of benediction to the previous chapters. The message of this book has been an effort to help God's people look beyond the present battle in all its subjective struggle. Through the surety of God's Word, we must fix our attention upon our sure victory. "What then, shall we say in response to this? If God is for us, who can be against us? . . . In all of these things we are more than conquerors through him who loved us" (Romans 8:31,37). Our battle with Satan's dark kingdom is really the Lord's battle. It's a battle that He has already won. It is a victory that He enables us to apply. We have all that we need to resist the enemy in every encounter that he directs against us. The daily aggressive application of our victory assures us of an invincible walk and the fulfillment of God's will.

In a few days, our daughter Judy returns from a year overseas as a missionary assistance worker. In *The Adversary,* I relate Judy's story and our family's direct battle with darkness. A bold confrontation with the powers of darkness was necessary to free her. Over ten years have passed since those days of trauma. She has graduated from high school and the Moody Bible Institute and has had time to mature and grow in grace. However, the years have not been free from attacks and struggles with Satan. Day by day there has been the necessity for spiritual warfare and the application of victory. There have been intense times when she has had to confront the enemy's efforts to intrude and rule her life.

I relate Judy's testimony because I want to stress again that the life of victory does not come with a "quick fix" of confrontation and one command for the enemy to leave. That may be necessary in intense times of battle, but that does not end the battle. Spiritual warfare is a daily walk, a consistent practice, a readiness to resist every day that we live.

I must also stress that a life of successful spiritual warfare does not guarantee a life without pain and disappointment. Viewed from the short perspective, there will be times when it seems that our enemy has won the day. Such limited sight does not tell the whole story, however. Paul's years of imprisonment at Caesarea and Rome must have seemed to the short-sighted to be a triumph for the enemy. Yet, during those years some of God's greatest victories over darkness were won. Paul's letters to the Ephesians, Philippians, and Colossians were all written from prison. He wrote Ephesians 6:10-18's message of victory, which has been shared through the centuries and around the world. Hold on to the vision of yourself as nothing but a winner.

ISBN: 978-0-8024-0143-4

The Adversary

The Christian Versus Demon Activity

The Bible plainly tells us that Satan schemes against us, that he wants to devour us, and that we struggle—not against the usual human enemies—but against Satan's highly organized kingdom. This battle will not go away. Ignoring it could be disastrous.

No enemy—not even Satan—is strong enough to overcome the God that lives in you. This best-seller will help you aggressively claim your triumph by relying on the almighty and powerful Word of God.

ISBN: 978-0-8024-9082-7

Preparing for Battle

A Spiritual Warfare Workbook

What if you knew someone was waiting for you, ready to attack? Wouldn't you do everything to protect yourself? Don't let Satan have victory in your life. God has given you an armory of weapons to use against the enemy. Find out how to fight him and win with this comprehensive workbook on spiritual warfare. Packed with real-life scenarios and revelation from God's Word, this workbook is ideal for groups, couples, families, and individual study.